MW00795476

AUTHENTIC CASE STUDIES

———

AUTHENTIC CASE STUDIES

Adolescence to Emerging Adulthood

First Edition

Kelli Jette, PhD

University of Cincinnati

SAN DIEGO

Bassim Hamadeh, CEO and Publisher
Amy Smith, Project Editor
Emely Villavicencio, Senior Graphic Designer
Sara Schennum, Licensing Associate
Natalie Piccotti, Director of Marketing
Kassie Graves, Vice President of Editorial
Jamie Giganti, Director of Academic Publishing

Copyright © 2020 by Cognella, Inc. All rights reserved. No part of this publication may be reprinted, reproduced, transmitted, or utilized in any form or by any electronic, mechanical, or other means, now known or hereafter invented, including photocopying, microfilming, and recording, or in any information retrieval system without the written permission of Cognella, Inc. For inquiries regarding permissions, translations, foreign rights, audio rights, and any other forms of reproduction, please contact the Cognella Licensing Department at rights@ cognella.com.

Trademark Notice: Product or corporate names may be trademarks or registered trademarks and are used only for identification and explanation without intent to infringe.

Cover image copyright © 2019 iStockphoto LP/Darwin Brandis; © 2013 iStockphoto LP/ Rangepuppies; © 2014 iStockphoto LP/Leontura; © 2018 iStockphoto LP/Stevanovicigor; © 2018 iStockphoto LP/Moussa81

Printed in the United States of America.

3970 Sorrento Valley Blvd., Ste. 500, San Diego, CA 92121

Thanks to B for the inside info—
you know who you are.

CONTENTS

INTRODUCTION

W orking with at-risk youth is not for the faint of heart. It is challenging and sometimes heartrending, while at other times rewarding and life changing. It requires a clear mind and objective perspective to offer clarity to those in need. Furthermore, practicing professionals need proper preparation to recognize factors contributing to deficits in good decision making and coping skills.

As the knowledgeable professional, you will be tasked in your future career with navigating the uncertainties of developing youth in today's fast-paced, multifaceted society. While overall development remains gradual, the youth of this generation are bombarded with constant stimuli that deeply affect their personal growth and maturation. It is necessary to equip yourself with pertinent knowledge about issues that affect youth today, as well as issues that have played important roles in developmental trends from the past.

To better prepare you for navigating the rocky roads of development, particularly with the adolescent and emerging adult populations, we have compiled a collection of case studies based on the true-life, authentic experiences of the youth of today. These case studies are the lived experiences of hundreds of people, relayed to the reader through their personal voices. Topics include substance abuse and exploration, sexual behavior, bullying and peer victimization, dietary and mental health disorders, depression, attention deficit and hyperactivity disorder, and a multitude of other behaviors that have proven potentially difficult for youth and emerging adults.

Be aware that these are personal and individual perspectives, with judgmental statements and conjecture in many cases. As an objective outsider, the reader may find flaws in the written word of these accounts. Lastly, what would you do if this were your child? The challenge is to identify the overt patterns that will emerge in an obvious manner and to delve deeply into the cases to analyze subthemes that include precursors and antecedents that manifest as dangerous or risk-taking behaviors.

Researchers state with certainty that empathy is a sophisticated skill that accompanies brain maturation. Thus as a practicing professional, it is important to remain professional, rely on and trust your intuition and training, and keep the human component at the forefront of your practice and pedagogy. The expertise you acquire now will grow exponentially and ultimately result in a rewarding career that will change the lives of those you serve.

As you read these real-life cases, please note that all names have been changed to protect anonymity. In addition, keep these guiding questions in mind as you analyze the cases:

- At what age did the detrimental behaviors manifest (present themselves), and how long have they persisted?
- What was the nature of the support systems around the struggling individual?
- Were there any particular triggers that may have diminished an otherwise healthy individual's coping skills?
- Were any systems (educational, family, peer, social, etc.) involved in the case?
- If you were privy to the situation, how would you, as a practicing professional, have gone about initiating an intervention?
- What do you think an appropriate intervention would look like?

TABLE OF CASE TOPICS

Case Study	Age	Disorder	Gender	Race/Ethnicity
1	14	Attention Deficit Hyperactivity Disorder (ADHD)	M	White
2	17	Lethargy	M	White
3	16	Drug Use	M	White
4	15	Drug Use	F	White
5	14	Oppositional Defiant Disorder (ODD)	M	White
6	13	Sexualized Behavior	F	White
7	15	ODD	M	White
8	15	Suicide	M	White
9	17	Alcohol	F	White
10	17	Alcohol	F	White
11	16	Sexualized Behavior	F	White
12	18	Drugs	M	White
13	15	Drugs and ODD	F	White
14	15	Drugs/Self-Harm	F	White
15	19	Drugs	F	White
16	12	ODD	F	White
17	12	ODD	M	White
18	13	ODD and Drugs	M	White
19	14	Self-Injury and ODD	F	Hispanic

Case Study	Age	Disorder	Gender	Race/Ethnicity
20	16	Smoking	F	White
21	16	Bullying/Drugs/Sex Orientation	M	White
22	16	Drugs	M	White
23	16	Drugs/ Delinquency	M	White
24	17	Depression/Drugs	M	White
25	14	Sexualized Behavior/ Drugs/ Depression	F	Black
26	15	Alcohol	M	White
27	18	Drugs/ODD	M	Black
28	12	ODD	M	Black
29	18	ODD	M	Black
30	19	Drugs/ODD/ Alcohol	M	White
31	15	ODD	F	White
32	17	Depression	M	Black
33	17	Sexualized Behavior	F	White
34	14	Drugs	M	White
35	13	Alcohol	M	White
36	14	ODD	M	White
37	12	Smoking/ODD/ Drugs	F	Black
38	14	ODD/Drugs	M	White
39	16	ODD/Drugs	M	White
40	12	ADHD/ODD	F	Black
41	11	ODD/Drugs	M	White
42	14	Drugs/Depression	M	White
43	13	Drugs	M	Black
44	13	ODD	M	Black
45	14	OPP/Drugs	F	Black
46	18	Depression/Drugs	F	White
47	13	Depression	F	White

Case Study	Age	Disorder	Gender	Race/Ethnicity
48	15	Drugs/ODD	M	Black
49	11	ODD	M	White
50	15	Drugs	F	White
51	17	Alcohol	M	White
52	12	Sexualized Behavior	F	White
53	17	Drugs/ODD	M	White
54	16	ODD	F	White
55	13	Bullying/ODD	M	Black
56	17	Depression	M	White
57	16	Bullying/Depression	M	White
58	14	Isolation/Drugs	M	White
59	16	ODD/Drugs	M	White
60	18	ODD/Drugs/Depression	M	White
61	15	Bullying/Drugs	M	White
62	13	ODD	M	White
63	16	Anxiety/ODD	M	White
64	17	ODD	M	White
65	17	Drugs	M	White
66	15	Suicide/Depression/Drugs/Sexualized Behavior	F	White
67	14	ODD	M	White
68	14	ODD	M	White
69	16	Sexualized Behavior/AIDS	F	Black
70	12	Bullying	M	White
71	15	Drugs/Sexualized Behavior	F	White
72	14	ODD/Aggression	M	White
73	16	Bullying/Drugs/Sexualized Behavior	F	White
74	15	Depression/ODD/Drugs	M	White
75	13	ODD	M	White

Case Study	Age	Disorder	Gender	Race/ Ethnicity
76	15	ODD	F	White
77	12	ODD	M	White
78	13	Sexualized Orientation/Drugs/Sexualized Behavior	F	White
80	12	Suicide/Drugs/ Sexualized Behavior	F	White
81	12	ODD/Abuse/Sexualized Behavior	F	White
82	14	ODD/Bullying	F	Black
83	13	Bullying	F	Black
84	16	Drugs	M	Black
85	11	Self-Injury/ Post-Traumatic Stress Disorder	M	White
86	12	Abuse	M	White
87	14	ODD/Bullying/ Aggression	F	Mixed
88	13	Drugs/Delinquency	M	White
89	14	Sexualized Behavior/Bullying	F	White
90	16	Sexual Orientation/ Suicide	M	White
91	18	Drugs	M	White
92	18	Drugs/Alcohol	F	White
93	19	Sexualized Behavior	F	White
94	19	Gambling Addiction	M	White
95	19	Drugs/Alcohol	F	White
96	19	Lethargy/Depression/Isolation/ Alcohol	F	White
97	20	Alcohol	M	Black
98	18	Drugs/Aggression	M	Black
99	17	Abuse/Pregnancy	F	Black
100	17	Drugs	M	White

JORDAN

I went to school with a peer we will call "Jordan." Jordan had major issues with being disruptive. He was constantly talking out and talking to other people, even when the teacher was lecturing. His mouth was never closed; he just did not seem to be able to stop talking. The teacher would ask him to be quiet and redirect him throughout every class. Jordan continued to be constantly disruptive. Jordan's behaviors caused him to get in trouble frequently, and he would receive several phone calls home and detentions, which never seemed to have any effect on stopping the disruptiveness. I recall numerous times that Jordan was asked to go sit out in the hallway by himself, where he would complete his work on his own. I always recall Jordan laughing about this. Perhaps it was defiance or maybe he was embarrassed. Either way, it appeared to other students that he absolutely didn't care and thought it was all a joke. Because this occurred on a daily basis, students felt it was annoying and unfair that they had to deal with the disruptive behaviors. It became a major annoyance and definitely affected Jordan's social well-being.

Looking back on Jordan's situation, I feel that the teacher should have recognized a more major problem that required intervention. Perhaps, the teacher could have provided him with positive attention. The teacher's attention was usually focused on the negative side of things, with consequences and punishments. Maybe the teacher should have acknowledged him before he had the chance to talk out of turn. The teacher and parents should have realized that there was a much more severe problem and maybe even sought help for Jordan with a counselor or psychologist. There definitely needed to be more analysis as to what was causing this problem in what seemed to be a normally developing teenager. Did he need to seek a physician for support? Did he have a disorder that caused his behaviors? Was he entering adolescence or having hormonal problems? Was this a factor for him? Overall, there could have been many factors that influenced his behaviors; therefore, I feel his parents and teacher should have met to devise a plan to help Jordan become successful in the classroom.

JON

A peer I recall from school was named "Jon." Jon always fell asleep in class, and he would snore loudly. He would snore so loudly that it became disruptive to the other students. Therefore, other students had trouble focusing, and Jon had trouble making passing grades in school. Before Jon would fall asleep in class, he would be on edge, acting irritable and rude to others. His peers would ask him a question, and he would reply in a very aggressive manner. He was always drowsy and rarely participated in class activities. After months of our teacher trying to keep him engaged and awake, she finally quit trying. She allowed him to make his own choice of sleeping and missing out on all classroom activities and lessons. I believe that there was much more to Jon's story. Instead of avoiding a conflict with Jon, the teacher should have stopped the sleeping. Perhaps she could have asked Jon why he isn't getting enough sleep at home and see what the schedule was like at his house. Perhaps bringing attention to the daily schedule could have opened a discussion regarding healthier habits. Did his parents keep him on a schedule or allow him to do what he wanted? Could depression or substance abuse problems be a factor? Stress? According to the textbook, "The family is a key part of the daily social context of adolescence in all cultures, but in most cultures, there are also profound changes in family relations from middle childhood to adolescence" (Jette and Killham, 2016, p. 40). Therefore, I feel Jon's family needed to be aware of his situation at school to help him be successful and to make sure that there weren't underlying physical or mental health issues causing Jon's unusual tiredness.

MIKE

"Mike" was in many of my classes in high school. Mike would come into class reeking of marijuana smoke. The marijuana smell would be so strong that students around him were constantly aware of it. The students regularly complained of suffering from headaches and clearly didn't want to sit near him; therefore, they would move their seats throughout the classroom. At times, I felt our teacher was completely aware of the situation and even heard about it through our chatter; however, she didn't want to confront Mike, considering he participated and always completed his work. I felt, as a student, that this was completely irresponsible for a teacher to disregard. I never witnessed any student go to the principal or resource officer about this problem. It was quite strange, in my opinion, that everyone recognized the problem with Mike, yet no individuals came forward to report the problem. In my opinion, I felt a peer could have helped Mike with his situation. Perhaps someone could have told him how the marijuana smoke affected him or her and how everyone could smell it. I think our teacher should have provided resources for Mike and discussed how drugs are illegal. Sending him to the counselor or contacting his parents could have assisted with the situation. The counselor or teacher could have also helped with the substance abuse he was experiencing. The textbook states, "In American society, substance use is rare before adolescence but fairly common by the end of secondary school" (Jette and Killham, 2016, p. 13). I feel substance abuse is increasing and more and more students are abusing drugs and alcohol at earlier ages.

ANONYMOUS PEER

One of my peers in high school experimented with marijuana and pills that she found in her parents' medicine cabinet. This behavior caused her to miss school on a regular basis. She did drugs because she wanted to fit in with her older friends and appear mature and sophisticated. She wanted them to be shocked that she could find drugs, and she wanted them to see her while she was high and acting in humorous and dangerous ways. It's possible she had low self-esteem and that being accepted by this older peer group helped her with her self-concept.

In my opinion, this child could have been helped with a supportive, personalized, and relevant learning environment. This type of support would have given the child a personal relationship with her teacher in which the teacher could have recognized that the child had issues with fitting in. The teacher could have contacted the parents, and as a team, they could have worked with the child on social skills that could have helped her develop a better self-concept (Arnette, 2016, p. 18).

OUTCAST FRIEND

I had a friend in middle school who regularly walked out in the middle of the school day and just went home. In my opinion, this friend always felt like an outcast, unwanted and unappreciated by our classmates and teachers. He always wanted to wear different clothing and be different than everyone else, sort of an anarchist attitude. Oddly, he also wanted to be accepted for the differences that he created in his individualism. The school reacted by putting him into in-school suspension regularly. This was the school's attempt to force him to be what they considered "normal," and, ultimately, this just exacerbated the problem by further isolating him and making him want to continue to leave the school grounds. Amazingly, he was a great student and enjoyed academic rigor. In-school suspension was not successful in keeping him from skipping class. All the continual suspensions did was negatively affect his grades.

To reach this student, I think a more flexible program might have been better for him. He needed flexibility in time and structure. Maybe half-day classes or a more challenging curriculum might have kept his interest in school. Perhaps even an online program that could be administered during the regular school day would have benefited him. This student went on to a career tech school and never skipped class at that institution. The middle school he went to had a criminal justice type of model where if you broke the rules, you paid the price without any regard for "why," and there was no individualization of education to help with those types of behavior problems (Arnette, 2016, p. 20).

SUFFOCATED STUDENT

A female peer from middle school who exhibited problems had extremely strict parents. They were so strict, in fact, that she felt suffocated. She would feel the need to lie about doing normal middle school activities and ultimately began experimenting with sex. She seemed like she wanted to have some sort of control over her life, and sexual encounters were something that made her feel wanted and in control. She was a great student, and she was even considered a "Goody Two-shoes" by her peers. Because of her hyperactive sexual encounters, she eventually ended up pregnant, and this caused her to miss a lot of school and eventually drop out.

In my opinion, this girl needed some freedom. She needed some space to allow her to learn how to make decisions rather than her extreme parents dictating her every single move. She needed an advocate to help her think about her future. It was easy for her to drop out and convenient at the time. Flexibility would have helped her, along with the assistance of an educational advocate. Teenagers tend to think about the present and not long term. They need helpful, nonjudgmental adults to assist them with decision-making processes.

In conclusion, educators and people who closely study education should know what keeps students from being delinquent. All of the students I think about who experienced problems and got offtrack had promise and possibilities. Positive reinforcements, rather than continual punishments, may have been a better option. This would include counseling and mental health services or support groups rather than suspensions, searches, police presence, and expulsions. Students with misbehaviors who have experienced suspensions and expulsions eventually give up and accept their labels because of a sense of helplessness. A more positive school environment is needed with flexibility and individualization.

MAGGIE

CASE

7

We will start with "Maggie." Maggie was someone I went to middle school and high school with but was never close to. I had interacted with her in large groups but never had an actual conversation with her. However, this did not affect how I witnessed one of the most drastic personality changes I've ever seen. In middle school, Maggie was a quiet, passive, shy girl who was easily overlooked. She was polite and kind; people never really talked about her because she never did anything dramatic worth mentioning. In high school, she had a long relationship (for high school) of over a year. They broke up about halfway through sophomore year, and everything changed. She went from quiet and polite to rude and obnoxious. She would act out in class, talking back to authority figures. She started dressing in all black, assumed a Gothic appearance, wore tons of makeup, and skipped class. At 15 years old, she would get drunk every weekend and do hard drugs with her friends from work. Maggie was very transparent about how she chose to live her life and would tell anyone who asked. She lost most of her friends from school because no one liked or agreed with the girl they now were presented with, and as a result, she only spent time with her work colleagues. She began dating a guy in his 20s (much older, not certain it was a legal relationship) and basically lived with him as a sophomore in high school. From what I know, her home life was never great with her parents, especially after their divorce. Her dad basically rejected her. Then her school life was ruined by the ending of her long-term relationship. I think these were major factors contributing to why her behavior changed so drastically in such a short amount of time. I don't know if anyone reached out to her or tried to help. She was very intimidating, and I wouldn't be shocked if she'd refused help, but I think that she definitely needed a good friend at that time, but I'm not certain she had anyone to turn to. The change was so obvious. I know teachers and other adults in her life would've noticed too. I think if someone would've genuinely reached out and tried to assist her, maybe things would be different. Currently, I still follow her on social media. She's still acting out, posting pictures of herself in lingerie or naked for all to see. She even offers herself to men for money. It's truly heartbreaking to see, but I think she thinks this is what she needs in her life to feel loved and to get approval from the world. I wish someone would have helped her years ago.

TIM

Let's talk about "Tim." A fair warning, this story has a tragic ending. Tim was someone that I went to high school with and knew prior, in middle school. He was best friends with my boyfriend in high school, so I knew him fairly well from hanging out and doing group activities. He was always the guy who could get a whole room to cry with laughter—a real comedian. He was friendly and kind, and good at making people feel like they mattered. He was the type of person who found joy in making people around him feel good about themselves. The first time I noticed that his behavior was changing was at the beginning of sophomore year. His innocent jokes took a very twisted turn into a dark sense of humor. These examples are very dark and offensive, but I think they're important to share to show how different of a person he had become. A student from a fellow high school in our district had recently committed suicide by hanging himself. Tim spray painted the school's rock with a picture of a hangman. I know. We were all shocked. Another example is when one of my best friends found out she had cancer. He made a twitter account called "_____'s Tumor" and tweeted, "Why isn't she dead yet?" The whole school was shocked by this. They tracked the IP address to his phone, and he was caught and suspended for a long time, and forced to write an apology to my friend and her family. I wish someone would've noticed the change or believed in Tim enough to realize that something must be seriously wrong for him to do this. I wish someone who had seen the tweet would've expressed to his parents that maybe there should be some concern regarding Tim's mental health. I wish one of his good friends would have tried to help instead of encouraging him in his twisted, scary actions. Instead, on March 20, 2014, Tim took his own life. We could have done better, and we should have done better. From that day on, the class of 2016 had an unmatchable bond. Even if we didn't particularly like someone, we were there for him or her if the person needed it because we couldn't go through another shocking heartbreak like that again. We couldn't lose another person in our "family," and so we fought through it together, and we became better at looking out for one another. Tim was one person we all knew, and it changed every single one of us for the remainder of our lives.

JAKE

"Jake" was one of Tim's best friends. I've known Jake since I was in elementary school. We grew up in the same classes and spent K–12th grade together. He was always popular, but also one of the smartest kids in school. He had the personality, the brains, and the leadership of a person you look at and know that one day he's going to do something special to change the world. Shortly after Tim's suicide, Jake started drinking and smoking weed every day. He skipped classes and started failing. One day, he got detention for skipping and literally brought vodka in a water bottle and got drunk during the school day while in the school suspension office. He seemed to have lost any sense of what he wanted in life and couldn't get himself out of the hole. Luckily, we learned from our mistakes, and people reached out to Jake and tried to help him. I definitely can't say we fixed him, or that his life was better, or that he stopped acting out. But at least he knew he had people who were in this thing with him, and he wasn't alone.

If there's anything I've learned from my high school experiences, it's that when people start acting out and doing very out-of-character things, it's a cry for help. We need to swallow our pride, get over the fear of being rejected, and reach out to these people: these friends, these students that we see so drastically changing before our eyes. Instead of sitting there later wishing that you would've done more, or done anything at all, you could end up saving a life.

CARRIE

M y sophomore year of high school began as expected, but quickly darkened as my peers and I began feeling an increasing pressure to engage in risky activities in order to be deemed "cool." This included attending parties, experimenting with drinking alcohol, and even engaging in some "minor" drug use. These activities were starting to become more common, and they only became more relevant as we grew up. Drinking and drugging soon became the norm for us when we told our parents we were just "hanging out." Engaging in such activities gave many of my fellow high schoolers a social edge. Being underage and partaking in what seemed like glamorous, adult activities made these people come across as more "mature" in the eyes of others our age. There was a certain interest in pursuing the unknown, the effects of partying, and trying and experimenting with new drugs, drinking, and sexual activities. I remember having a fear that I would be considered "lame" if I didn't partake or at least know about these types of behaviors. As time passed, however, I realized that those who engrossed themselves in these undertakings were only putting themselves in danger and jeopardizing their futures. While many of my peers were able to overcome their bad habits before it was too late, there were many others whose lives were affected by their poor decisions.

One such peer who stands out to me is a girl in my class whom I will refer to as "Carrie." Carrie was in the popular circle and had a lot of loyal "followers." Before getting herself into trouble, Carrie was a bubbly, bright individual. She was extremely friendly and outgoing, which caused her to gain these "followers" in the first place. She had an older brother who commonly participated in risky behaviors, and she had divorced parents who were pretty lax/permissive and didn't enforce many rules upon either

Carrie or her brother. On the weekends, Carrie was able to host parties with alcohol supplied by her older brother. She would invite only her close friends, and they would boast endlessly at school about their drunken escapades. She made drinking look cool, at first. Over time, however, she began to gain a significant amount of weight from heavy drinking. She started to fall behind in school because she wasn't completing her assignments on time. Eventually, I would find out that she received a "driving under the influence" charge and lost her driving privileges for a year. By this time, she had lost many of her friends who couldn't keep up or refused to partake in these activities with her, as they were affecting their lives as well. Her parents, while not strict, were affected nonetheless by her decisions. They had to pay for Carrie's legal fees and were held partially responsible every time one of Carrie's friend's parents found out about her parties. When the school contacted her parents regarding her poor grades, Carrie's parents had to deal with that as well. I believe that the social pressures to be liked by her peers led Carrie down that destructive path.

ANN

One of my high school peers became involved in risky behavior. "Ann" was actually one of my closest friends at the time, so I witnessed her behavior and the consequences firsthand, with an uncomfortable close-up view. She never felt attractive and was never very confident around guys, but when she became close friends with one of her field hockey teammates, she started to learn how to get male attention through her appearance and actions. I might add that these appearance changes and actions were not healthy or what I would consider attractive. One of her teammates was very promiscuous with boys and often participated in sexual activities that were what I considered "abnormal" for high school–aged "kids." On the weekends, the hockey teammate took Ann to parties and introduced her to a plethora of guys. It was only a matter of a few weeks before Ann began engaging in sexual activities that quite often involved very adult scenarios and with many different boys. Ann and her teammate friend refused to have one boyfriend and hated the idea of monogamy, but rather "hooked up" with various and random guys. Ann's close friends, including myself, felt betrayed as she began to spend less and less time with us. She often lied to her parents about where she was going and who she was with, which strained her relationship with her parents. She habitually invested herself in the guys she would hook up with and would get heartbroken when they wouldn't reciprocate emotionally. Psychologically, she was damaged. She acted as though the only way to be appreciated by a boy was to provide unlimited sexually charged experiences. If a guy showed even the slightest amount of sexual interest in her, her mood would skyrocket. It was like she needed validation, and without that validation, she would plummet into the depths of despair. She was caught in a never-ending cycle of sexual escapades that led nowhere until she met her first boyfriend, who finally shared her feelings of investment and taught her what it was like to be in a healthy relationship. When Ann was able to learn her true value, her risky behaviors came to an end, thankfully.

MAX

A peer of mine ventured into some extremely risky behavior in late high school, which I believe had a significant effect on his life today, as well as his future. "Max" had always been one step ahead of everyone else. He wasn't particularly athletic, smart, good-looking, or popular, but he had a desire to be known for something. I speculate that this is what led him to delve into the world of drugs. He started, as so many do, with weed and quickly became branded as a "stoner." However, eventually (and quite quickly) this wasn't enough, and Max soon began experimenting with other drugs, particularly prescription pills. He started taking Xanax recreationally and became notorious for "popping pills." He lost interest in his extracurricular activities as well as his friends and isolated himself. It was as if all he cared about was getting high, to the point that he just sat on a couch and nodded off alone in his basement. He skipped school regularly and rarely completed assignments, which caused his grades to fall drastically. Max got in trouble quite often at school and with law enforcement for his risky (not to mention illegal) behaviors. These altercations not only affected Max and his future but also took a toll on his parents as well. He was only accepted into a few colleges, and while he enrolled in one, he was still deep into an addiction that went on to affect his college career.

A lot of my peers seem to have been driven toward risky behaviors by a societal pressure to be a certain person or to act a certain way. Glamorous, sophisticated drug use that has been seen in our culture made a lot of my friends attempt to emulate these behaviors. Identity formation and self-esteem seem to play a large role in choosing whether or not to engage in these activities. While it can be done, stopping these behaviors or breaking these habits once they are already in motion can be a difficult task. Prevention, on the other hand, is much more feasible and can help in avoiding these behaviors (and their consequences) in the first place. For a lot of kids, their parents could have been a little stricter or at least warned them of the dangers of underage drinking (and drinking in general), engaging in sexual activities at a young age, or experimenting with recreational drugs. Friends could have offered help or pointed out that their behavior seemed dangerous and was starting to affect their lives. While these actions were not guaranteed to help, stop, or prevent people from engaging in risky activities, they could have made a difference.

PASSED AWAY PARENT

When a parent passes away, it can affect our friends differently—especially in high school. One of my high school peers showed risk-taking behavior after the student's parent passed away. Prior to this happening, the student was at the top of the class and was always a really hardworking and studious person. The person was always present at school and constantly involved in activities at school and in many sports groups. After the passing of the parent, the student began to not show up to school regularly and no longer cared about grades. The student quit all of the clubs and sports teams, and eventually ended up going from straight As in school to getting Cs and Ds—barely getting by academically. The student began going out often and coming to school under the influence of a variety of alcohol and drug combinations. The student would often have aggressive outbursts in class toward teachers and other students when asked to do something the student didn't want or feel like doing, or if another classmate would say something the person didn't like. I think the counselors and school psychologist should have intensely followed up to help this student—the teachers and the counselors should have done more than what I witnessed. There was an obvious and major shift in behavior before and after the student's parent died, and the person was obviously hurting. I think that teachers should have talked to the student and let my peer know that they were there for the student. I also think they could have gotten the counselors involved to talk to my peer as well and potentially place the student in services and support groups to support the peer through that difficult and sad time. It still amazes me that no professional/adult at school or, apparently, in the household recognized the self-destructive behaviors of a teenager in mourning over the death of a parent.

SELF-HARM

A peer that I went to high school with experienced drastic changes after the end of an intimate relationship. When the break up occurred, the person turned to drugs and alcohol to self-soothe. The person began to party on a regular basis—any chance the peer could get—and started using drugs. Most alarming was when the peer began to self-harm when the previous partner began a new relationship. I think that when our peer group noticed the drastic and dangerous changes, we should have said something to someone who had more authority than us, perhaps the student's parents, our own parents, or teachers or counselors. I think that another method that could have helped the student would have been having more drug prevention at the high school level rather than at the middle school level. I can only speak from my personal experience at school, but the drug experimentation and usage did not get very intense until high school. I feel that the school resources were misdirected at the wrong age group. As stated in the book, "Tweens and Teens: A Human Development Perspective," there are school-based adolescent substance abuse/use prevention programs and drug testing that can be used to keep students away from drugs (Jette & Killham, 2016). Another resource that I think could have been useful to the student is multimodal programs. In the book, "Tweens and Teens: A Human Development Perspective" it states, "Multimodal programs ... provide service to students, families, and educators. Others focus on changing the community and the environment" (Jette & Killham, 2016). I think that programs like this could help students because it shows different perspectives of each situation, how to deal with the situation, and how to help the student instead of just focusing solely on the student, plus it makes certain that the environment is a good place for the student as well.

COLLEGIATE FREEDOM

The most memorable peer to me who showed at-risk behavior is a peer I went to school with all of my life, and we continued to the same college. In primary, middle, and high school, this peer was a student with very strict parents. As a family, they rarely went out and spent all of their time focusing on school and clubs that they were involved in. This peer was never a person to drink or use drugs, because if the student's parents had found out, it would have been very bad for my peer. When this peer went to college and for the first time experienced freedom. The student started going to parties and drinking. Most recently, the student has started using marijuana on a regular basis, and my peer told me about not caring that much about school and getting good grades anymore.

I think that it is important that drug prevention initiatives continue into higher education and not just in middle and high school. When college students no longer have parents controlling them as much, and more freedom occurs, it can be easier for them to do things they wouldn't have done before. In college, there are things that campuses can do, like banning drug use and smoking on campus, having health and counseling/psychological services on campus, and offering drug- and alcohol-free recreational activities (Jette & Killham, 2016). I believe that this can be useful to help students stay away from drug use and abuse. The book also states, "In addition, student health and wellness programs should be implemented, focusing on changing campus attitudes toward drug use, identifying students at highest risk for abuse, and providing assessments and intervention services when appropriate" (Jette & Killham, 2016).

I feel that it is important for colleges to train professors to identify when students are at risk, because students may not always want help with drug use and won't seek help themselves. Noticing when students may be abusing drugs and doing something about it can be important so that students are still getting the help they need, even if they do not want the help at that time. Awareness of psychological issues is imperative.

JACK

A ge 11 is when I began to experience many puberty-related changes. So did many of my peers. Along with puberty-related changes came mental, emotional, and physical changes that truly affected all of us. Most of the time, these changes sent us for a loop and were oftentimes uncontrollable. Middle school created aggressive attitudes and behavioral problems. Our middle school was directly connected to an elementary school that I had attended from kindergarten to eighth grade. I never was a troublesome student. "Jack" attended our school from sixth to eighth grade. Jack was always suspended, involved in fighting, or sent home for failing to follow the teacher's directions. Jack was seen by our peers as more of a "class clown" and did not take anything seriously, as if he had no care for anything school related. Jack's risky behaviors resulted in him being retained and having to retake the eighth-grade year. I am sure this was a very negative setback for Jack and may have been disappointing. We have discussed the damaging effects of holding students back after the third-grade year. Statistics show that retaining students after the third-grade year does little or nothing for the student academically and actually does more harm than good. Luckily, Jack began to take his classes and coursework seriously, and he graduated high school successfully. I believe that Jack was unaware of the consequences of his behaviors, and once he was, he corrected his attitude. This should have been brought to his and his family's attention earlier to keep the eighth grader from being retained. Obviously, this was an attention-seeking behavior that could have been fixed much sooner and prevented the extra remediation year.

TARYN

"Taryn" attended our school from kindergarten to seventh grade and was in continual trouble, or what we viewed as turmoil. Taryn received multiple in-school and home suspensions before his parents determined that a regular public school environment might not be the place where he could flourish. In eighth grade, Taryn was transferred to a different, yet neighboring, middle school, and his risky behaviors slowly came to a halt. Upon entering high school, Taryn participated in sports and worked with his mentors to maintain good grades. Amazingly, Taryn is now in college, playing football on a partial scholarship, and on a path to a better and stable lifestyle. I believe that his parents' decision to change Taryn's school was very significant and helped him in his future endeavors. This demonstrates the power of a strong support system and parents who are present in the lives of their teenagers. Sometimes admitting that there is a problem and attempting to fix the negative issue by thinking "out of the box" is a very strategic and helpful means of assisting troubled teenagers.

CHAD

" Chad" began attending Longworth in the eighth grade. On his first day, we noticed that there was something very different about Chad. He was wearing a police-issued ankle bracelet and had a tattoo on his forearm. These two factors were very shocking to my peers and I because none of us had tattoos and never really participated or even knew about risky behaviors—especially behaviors so severe that they resulted in house arrest. However, we were all completely curious as to what he'd done to be placed on house arrest, especially at a middle school age. There was plenty of pre-teen conjecture as to what terrible acts Chad had committed. While attending our school, he was very quiet and socially awkward, but constantly in trouble and being punished by our teachers and school staff. He never wanted to follow the teachers' directions and was continually removed from class and sent to the principal's office.

Eventually, as the third quarter arrived, Chad was suspended for fighting and a more severe issue: possession of drugs in his book bag. Chad was quickly expelled from our school. A lot of students were surprised that he'd had drugs in his possession because we did not participate in such activities and risky behaviors, and were blissfully unaware of such problems at that age. I never saw Chad again after his expulsion and always wondered if things ever changed for him. However, I believe that the environment that Chad experienced at home, especially, is what motivated the risky behaviors that he participated in. We could only wonder what was going on with his parents and family and home life. I believe that Chad's home environment may have been problematic, resulting in increased risk-taking behaviors. We were not certain that Chad had a stable situation.

MIA

Unfortunately, I have known many peers in my life who have demonstrated at-risk behaviors in and out of the school setting. One of these peers was "Mia." She and I went to elementary and middle school together. Her most disturbing at-risk behavior included extreme picking at her fingernails until they would bleed—almost borderline self-harm—not turning her homework in, and verbally bullying her classmates. I honestly felt that I was a target of this verbal abuse and was definitely intimidated by her aggression. I recall that between kindergarten and second grade, Mia never exhibited aggressive behaviors, and we were close playmates and friends. It changed in the third grade when Mia started exhibiting her risk-taking, negative behaviors. I believe the illness that Mia's father contracted was a major problem. Her father spent months in a hospital, which I feel started the downward spiral of negative behaviors for Mia. I believe it was the anxiety and isolation or loneliness that resulted in the nail picking, self-harm, and verbal abuse toward others. Mia was most likely acting out of fear regarding her father's well-being and just didn't know how to show this properly. Her cruelty to her peers was a cry for help, and it needed to be dealt with by more knowledgeable adults.

Mia's peers, including me, could have assisted in her situation by reaching out to her and asking her if she wanted to hang out or play with us, instead of only isolating her more when she began to use mean words and bully us. We were so young. This would not have been a natural or apparent reaction to a peer who was being so vicious to us. Had we been more mature, including Mia would have made her feel more accepted and like she had friends and peers to lean on. I also believe our teachers should have been more understanding with Mia, instead of fixating on her publicly in front of the entire class when she would not turn in her homework, which I feel further damaged her self-esteem. Obviously, that type of "public shaming" is not even a legal educational practice anymore and should be avoided. Private meetings between teachers and Mia would have benefited her much more in that scenario.

CADEN

A peer who began to exhibit risk-taking behaviors was a good friend of mine in high school named "Caden." During Caden's freshman and sophomore years, she was consistent and performed at A and B levels. In addition, Caden was very kind to others and very much involved with the theater department at our school. However, during her junior year, Caden began to use a Juul and then marijuana. While this did not affect her kind personality, it did cause her to begin struggling in school, and we noticed that she seemed to have lost interest in her friends and the theater department. I believe that what caused her to disengage from positive things and to begin engaging in these risk-taking activities was the stress of her parents getting divorced. This divorce caused Caden to have more responsibility in caring for her younger siblings.Caden's parents could have assisted her recognizing that the divorce was a huge change for herand that she may have needed to start seeing a counselor to talk through this familial problem and to develop healthy habits for dealing with the new change instead of drugs.

CASE

ABE

21

A peer who developed risk-taking behavior was "Abe." Abe was a friend and peer of mine as early as middle school. He was an excellent student. Problems arose when he became a victim of bullying in the later part of our middle school years. Abe was bullied solely because of his homosexuality. His family was also very conservative, so they were not supportive of Abe's homosexuality; therefore, they were not helping him with the bullying problem or even empathizing with Abe. Because of this, Abe turned to drinking as a way to escape his problems. Because of the drinking, Abe did not want to socialize with his friends (me included) anymore. A way that Abe's parents could have assisted in his situation was by being supportive of him rather than treating him differently because of his sexual orientation. Abe's teachers could have been more proactive by leading positive discussions about sexual orientation and having a zero-tolerance policy when it came to the bullying. Abe eventually graduated, and I understand that he is doing well. Hopefully, the aging process and gaining independence throughout high school, along with so many anti-bullying and pro-sexual orientation movements, helped Abe to overcome the difficulties he was having in school and among his family.

MY OLD CRUSH

22

I had a crush on a boy in my grade during my middle school years. He was on the football team and would occasionally get in minor trouble at school, but nothing serious. This boy continued to get in increasingly more trouble, and it became alarming. As a result, my crush inevitably faded as we entered high school. First, the boy began to fail in school and received extremely poor grades. In addition, the boy began to "party" a lot, and by that I mean drinking and smoking marijuana on a regular basis. He took part in what the textbook defines as "social substance use," which "involves the use of substances during social activities with one or more friends" (Jette & Killham, 2016, p. 14). While the definition implies that it was perhaps occasional usage or weekend usage, it was actually daily usage with friends from what my peers and I considered a "bad crowd." These behaviors resulted in him failing school-issued drug tests, which caused him to get his driving privileges revoked and ended his football participation. The most recent news I heard about this boy was a terrible incident in which he burglarized a home with a group of friends and got arrested. The textbook talks about how delinquent crimes "usually take place in a group" (Jette & Killham, 2016, p. 52).

HEART SURGEON

Delinquent behavior was demonstrated by a boy who went to my school as soon as high school began. This boy was in academically advanced courses and cared very much about his grades and his college future; he had the ambition of becoming a heart surgeon. This boy began drinking and smoking marijuana recreationally with his friends, or, as it is commonly referred to, he took part in "social substance use." Moreover, this boy, who had always been super kind to everyone, started acting cruel to others and became what I considered a jerk. He began to always make fun of people and seemed to only care about himself. Tragically, whether the drug usage was partly or mostly to blame, this boy was accused of raping a girl at a party during our senior. Although he was never found guilty, in my opinion, this accusation aligned with his behavior at that time.

The boy could have been helped in numerous ways. There should have been an intervention. It was obvious that something was amiss when the strong student began to fumble with coursework and grades. Also, there was such an abrupt personality change, I find it hard to believe that the adults (teachers/parents) did not recognize this as a red flag signaling that something deeper was going on. The parents should have monitored him more closely and should have attempted to at least regulate the alcohol and substance use, if not send him to rehabilitation. It is extremely difficult to make it impossible for a teen to take part in substance use; however, from an outsider's perspective, the parents should not have been enablers, always making excuses for their son or covering up the substance abuse issues and ignoring them. Also, in an ideal world, the friends should have discouraged him rather than *encouraged* him to drink and do drugs. Lastly, I do think the school took the correct action in attempting to deal with delinquent students, specifically those who use substances. My school often issues drug tests. If students test positive, they get privileges taken away like driving and playing sports, while also having to attend a class and counseling about abusing substances. This would scare my peers into not partying because they did not want these privileges taken away.

MY LITTLE BROTHER

Unfortunately, I have a very personal view of someone exhibiting risk-taking behavior; within the past few years, my brother, who is two years younger than me, has chosen to cope with a family incident in very harmful ways. It all started when he began to isolate himself and avoid our family. He remained cooped up in his room and disengaged from our typical, normal family activities. We also noticed that he started a bad habit that was unlike him, which was binge drinking on the weekends. A short time after we noticed this behavior change, the smell of marijuana could be detected coming from his room on a regular basis. Furthermore, when my family decided to move to a new home, his drinking seemed to stop, but his weed use escalated to the point of being a constant issue. I privately inquired why he was partaking in these bad habits, and he told me that it helped to alleviate his anxiety. To which I asked, "What are you anxious about?" He could not define the reason.

Lately, my brother sleeps all day and has been skipping school so much that it has become problematic for his grade point average. His behavior has led me to believe that he is experiencing some form of depression. The textbook explains that one of the most common causes of depression is "conflict with friends and family" (Jette and Killham, 2016, p. 55). This makes sense for my brother, as I think his depressed mood and unhealthy coping mechanisms came directly after a family incident that split a lot of us up. Family issues can be very difficult to handle, and he is obviously not handling this family crisis in a healthy way.

It seems easy to say what family and friends should do to help a person, but it is a lot harder when you are *a part* of the family and friends who should be helping. I think there is a lot my family could have done or could be doing that would help my brother, but they, including me, have been too focused on their own problems. Currently, my mother is trying to arrange a time for her and my dad to sit down and talk to my brother about what exactly is going on. My brother is a difficult person to talk to because he has a lack of care about his life and shows little sign of actually *wanting* to get better, so I understand why my parents have been hesitant to do this. My brother is a smart young man with lots of potential, and I do believe that he will eventually get better. He has the goal of going to college to pursue engineering because despite skipping a lot of school, he still gets great grades thanks to the leniency of his teachers. I am really hoping that when he goes to college next year, he will be able to heal and realize that he can do a lot more with his life than smoke marijuana in his bedroom.

DATING A MARRIED MAN

My friend growing up in school was heavy as well as fully developed. She was outgoing but was not in what was considered the "popular crowd." We became friends because I was not in the popular crowd either, so we gravitated toward one another in some of our classes. There are blessings to be had by not being invited into a clique, and our friendship was one of them. She was very mature and advanced for our age. She began having sex at the age of 14 with an older married man she met through another friend. I know this was not legal, and the older married man could have been easily arrested. She would skip school and go to this man's house. On one occasion, she begged me to go with her to the older man's house. So, trying to be as adventurous as she was, I skipped school with her, and the guy picked us up—again totally illegal. While I was there, he offered us alcohol, which I did not partake in. But? My friend did drink some, and she smoked marijuana with the older married man. When I think about this situation now, I think of all the things that could have happened to us and shake my head at myself. My friend started missing more school, and she refrained from talking to me much after the visit. This is because I kept hounding her to stop seeing the older married guy. Her parents found out eventually, and she ran away for a while and finally dropped out of school. There were several risk factors with this situation—actually, it was extremely dangerous and completely illegal. Skipping school was bad; my friend having unprotected sex in a dangerous relationship was worse, and an unintended result was that she started drinking alcohol and doing drugs at an abusive level and dropped out of school—the rock bottom for a teenage girl, I suppose. I wish she could have gone to the counselors at school, maybe they could have helped her or gotten her on the right track for some help when she was younger. I talked to her some time later. She had been diagnosed with depression. We probably could compare her experience to the fact that young girls who develop early can be shown statistically to have more problems because of a lack of mental maturity and often being accepted by an older crowd, which in this case caused my friend to be easily led into substance abuse and sexual activity.

ZAC

I was very close to "Zac" growing up. Unfortunately, Zac started drinking at a young age. Perhaps he is an example of genetic substance addiction. However, he ended up becoming an alcoholic and drank for most of his adult years. Zac just quit abusing alcohol a few years ago because of major health issues. Zac was a happy kid and well-liked by his peers. He was not a good student, most likely because of his dyslexia and maybe some other special learning needs that were not necessarily recognized during that time period. It literally only took one offering of alcohol: Zac was offered alcohol by an older guy his older sister was dating, and he never recovered. Zac never came back from it. The alcohol took ahold of him quickly and in a very severe way. Once he started full-fledge drinking, he was a totally different person. Zac was argumentative and a sloppy drunk. It was difficult and disappointing to be around him. He dropped out of school at age 16. His father was a functioning alcoholic and had passed away at age 49 from complications due to alcoholism. My friend had a rough adult life, and I think about what a different life he could have had if he'd gotten help when he was young. He needed an individualized education plan IEP for academic help, which we do now in our schools. He should have been placed in some type of rehab and counseling, probably AlA Teen would have helped a lot (Killham, 2017).

CHRISTIAN STUDENT

I knew a sincere Christian boy growing up in a small high school. He was unpopular, nerdy, and quite heavyset, which people often teased him about. His father had not been in his life since he was a very young boy. As soon as he graduated from high school, he got a job at a fast-food restaurant, where he had requested Sundays off for church attendance. It was not long after he started working that he fell in with a bad crowd and started making bad decisions to impress his new friends with whom he worked. He quit going to church and made the horrible decision to follow in his new friends' footsteps. He helped his friends break into the fast-food restaurant, although he was lucky and never was convicted on any charges having to do with the break-in. (They did not get any money.) He went so far as to steal his mother's rent money from her bank account one day to give to his friends, who most likely needed money for drugs. He started taking amphetamine pills to keep himself alert, and then he ended up in the hospital a few times for dehydration because of the pills' side effects. His mother determined that she could no longer help him because he would not listen to her and would become enraged and belligerent. His mother sent him to live in another state with his aunt, uncle, and cousins. His uncle and cousins spent a lot of time with him and have made every effort to make him feel like part of the family. This was a key element to his improvement. He is doing really good for the moment, and he has seen a doctor who has diagnosed him with being bipolar disorder. This young man had developed major issues throughout his teenage and early adulthood years, and he was obviously trying to fit in somewhere. Because he felt different, he was vulnerable to negative peer influences, and he definitely needed some mental health assistance.

ROBBING FORT KNOX

A memory that has always haunted me, even into adulthood, was the year my teacher labeled my class "the worst sixth-grade class" in her teaching career. I vividly recall this statement because she repeated it on a regular basis. The teacher even brought the principal into our classroom to reiterate this statement. This memory has followed me because I felt blamed and inaccurately labeled—I was never a troublemaker during any grade level of school and had the behavior record to prove it. My best friend was the student council body president, and I always tried my best to show teachers that I was paying attention. I do recall some of my classmates' antics and what they did to make the teachers and principals react the way they did. I felt unfairly accused because I was vigilant in my attempts to remain innocent and only tried to keep company with the best-behaved students, which often caused me to be teased. I still resisted. I felt that the administrators unfairly grouped me with the guilty parties.

In particular, one classmate of mine who socialized with some of the "cooler" kids in school had a reputation for being embarrassingly blunt or straightforward in his comments. This boy had an older brother who was always in trouble with school officials and police. On one occasion, the younger boy, who was in my class, took notice that the teacher had a miserable head cold and wasn't performing at the "top of their teaching game." My classmate took this as an opportunity to crawl out of the window and leave class. I know that he did this because most of his clique was watching him, and he felt it would be an impressive misbehavior to the rest of his peers. It would be the first time any of them had ever jumped out of a window during class. He did, indeed, leave via a window but returned later—with a mischievous look as though he had just gotten away with robbing Fort Knox—because, quite frankly, the teacher did not realize that he was gone. He was disappointed when the teacher did not comment; he wanted the teacher to reprimand him.

Physically, there were no warning signs or changes in this boy, other than the fact that he and his posse had shorter hair during their years of delinquent actions. A way that this student could have been assisted is by being given more attention, or at least recognition, because it seemed like that was all he was looking for. He was a younger brother, and he seemed to always want attention whether it was good or bad. Attention-seeking behaviors can ultimately cause immature preteens and teens to develop bad habits, and entice them into dangerous, thrill-seeking behaviors that can cause lifelong issues if not addressed and ceased early in life.

CHRIS

CASE

29

M y classmate, "Chris," exhibited delinquent behavior as early as his elementary and middle school years. Chris's behavior got steadily worse until the final year of high school when it was the worst. Chris would blurt out undesirable comments at his peers, in and out of class. The worst episode with Chris was an incident when he went to the elementary school and defecated on one of the playground slides. I think that Chris wanted to fit into his negative peer group so badly that he would do anything extreme to warrant their admiration—to him, he exhibited this delinquent behavior for acceptance from the other students. He needed to wear glasses, but he refused to wear them until his sophomore year in high school in an attempt to protect his image from being "uncool." I believe that if Chris was assisted by a counselor to help him with his behaviors, maybe he would have avoided the major delinquent acts he did in middle school and high school. Teachers should realize that there is often a group of students who are feeding off each other to take risks, and they should try to diffuse the situations. This is often referred to as a contagion, and the peer pressure is often so intense that great kids turn to attention-seeking bad behavior to impress those peers.

At the very end of our high school career, Chris found a girlfriend, and he seemed to clean up his act moving towards college. Interestingly, I think once he realized that he did not have to be "cool" in front of peers, and was accepted in a monogamous and healthy relationship, he started to realize the error of his prior ways.

CASE 29

CHRIS

My classmate, "Chris," exhibited delinquent behavior as early as his elementary and middle school years. Chris's behavior got steadily worse until the final year of high school when it was the worst. Chris would blurt out undesirable comments at his peers, in and out of class. The worst episode with Chris was an incident when he went to the elementary school and defecated on one of the playground slides. I think that Chris wanted to fit into his negative peer group so badly that he would do anything extreme to warrant their admiration—to him, he exhibited this delinquent behavior for acceptance from the other students. He needed to wear glasses, but he refused to wear them until his sophomore year in high school in an attempt to protect his image from being "uncool." I believe that if Chris was assisted by a counselor to help him with his behaviors, maybe he would have avoided the major delinquent acts he did in middle school and high school. Teachers should realize that there is often a group of students who are feeding off each other to take risks, and they should try to diffuse the situations. This is often referred to as a contagion, and the peer pressure is often so intense that great kids turn to attention-seeking bad behavior to impress those peers.

At the very end of our high school career, Chris found a girlfriend, and he seemed to clean up his act moving towards college. Interestingly, I think once he realized that he did not have to be "cool" in front of peers, and was accepted in a monogamous and healthy relationship, he started to realize the error of his prior ways.

63

BRYCE

T he classmate that I would like to talk about was one of my closest
friends, who did not start exhibiting delinquent behavior until after
his high school years. We will refer to him as "Bryce." Bryce's father was
the dean of students at our high school, so Bryce's home life was extremely
strict. Bryce was always on time for school and was intensely pressured
by his parents to succeed in school. As soon as Bryce went to college, he
had no one monitoring his work ethic in school or even his attendance
in classes. Bryce constantly attended parties and experimented with
things that he would have never done in high school: binge drinking,
trying hard drugs, sex with random people. Bryce had a very hard time
adapting to this newfound freedom in his first year of college and exhibited every delinquent behavior one should typically avoid. I have lost
close contact with him over the last few years, and I feel that he needs a
friend or someone to help push him to do well in school. A counselor or
another adviser from his school could also have helped him make goals,
make better decisions, and stay focused on the tasks he needed to complete during his freshman year. I do not feel that his parents recognized
his off-putting behaviors. I think they believed that he was succeeding
when he was not. Acquaintances have informed me that Bryce is doing
much better now that we are in our final years of college. Bryce even
adopted a dog, which I think is helping him to maintain responsibility
and emotional stability.

All of my classmates whom I have witnessed go on a downward spiral
of delinquent behavior could have been helped by a counselor or a
teacher who really connected with them. I believe that all students can
be good and successful students; it just depends on what the students

may need to help them enjoy and engage in their personal learning. Most students seem to understand that they need to be more respectful as they mature, but it is important for students to grasp this concept before things get out of hand.

DIVORCE TURMOIL

A friend I went to school had a major change in behavior because of a trauma she was experiencing in her life. Her parents had initiated a divorce, and this caused a lot of emotional turmoil in her life at the time. She had always been very immersed in school academics and extracurricular activities. Suddenly, she was not turning in homework assignments, not going to her classes, and not attending any of her required sporting events. I do not feel that many people were aware of her turmoil and negative behaviors at the time. She was a private person normally, and she didn't share her personal life with many people on a regular basis. If she had been more open with people like her teachers and coaches, they would have been more understanding of her life situation and could have found ways to help. My friend went from having all As to almost failing a class. This was extremely shocking and unlike her in every way. She expressed (to me) that her parents accused her of being rebellious and overly dramatic. The parents failed to recognize how the divorce was negatively affecting her and her life. They were furious about her poor grades and disconnection from school activities. I know that if her parents would have more actively acknowledged that the divorce was creating her negative mental and emotional state, things could have been different for her. While she finally ended up being okay and returning to her typical self, I know she went through some dark times in her life that could have been less traumatic.

SECRET LIFE

A person I knew at school, but wasn't necessarily friends with, was a textbook definition of a bully, and I honestly was afraid of this person. This person was extremely mean and seemed perpetually angry. He would publicly lash out at teachers and other students, and would intentionally start fights for no reason. At first, I thought he just enjoyed the attention he got from acting out and being in trouble, keeping his image as a tough guy. It finally culminated when he was suspended for a fight in the cafeteria. It was then that I realized there were underlying reasons for his violent and aggressive behaviors. I was at a grocery store, and the boy was working there. He was checking me out, and he asked me if anything exciting had happened at school while he had been gone. I nervously said, "No," and explained that it was just the same redundant day-to-day routine. He began to share with me about his mom leaving the family and that it was just him and his dad now living together, that his dad was an alcoholic, that he had to take care of his dad, and that he could barely keep food on the table. It was heartbreaking. I could not believe this person, who was always so intimidating, was opening up to me. He told me that he was relieved and happy that he was suspended so he could get more hours at work. The reasons for his outbursts began to become crystal clear to me. I felt bad for him because I don't think many people knew what his home life was like and never took the time to try to understand him—not that they could, as he never acted anything but aggressive toward people, so, naturally, our peers avoided him. Since that grocery store incident, I would never say we were "friends," but we were acquaintances, and I made special (private) efforts to check up on him from time to time to see how he was doing.

When younger adolescent children are forced to mature and handle things before they are ready, like in this situation, I feel that it affects people differently and potentially in a negative way. I think had people, peers, and teachers understood or taken the time to get to know more about my classmate and his life, they would have been more sympathetic to his behaviors. I think teachers and/or administration should have either known about, or found out about, his home life. One lingering question I have about the situation is if they (teachers and administrators) did know about the situation, why weren't they more supportive in taking action to help him?

DAWN

A person who ran into problems was someone who was a best friend that I eventually drifted away from. We will call her "Dawn." Dawn started dating someone new, and their relationship got way too serious, way too quickly. Friends and I planned an intervention to discuss with her how quickly the relationship was moving. Dawn accused us of being jealous of her and her relationship, which was not the case but apparently a normal reaction in many interventions. Soon after, Dawn stopped talking to not only me but also our other friends. It was as if she became obsessed with her relationship and didn't care about anything else. I am still baffled by this situation. How can best friends drift apart over a boy or even the mention of the inappropriateness of the relationship? Later in their love affair, Dawn ended up breaking off their engagement because of a physical abuse occurrence that ended with her having a massive black eye. Unfortunately, the situation had to escalate to such a terrible pinnacle for her to realize that her judgment was not clear and the relationship was not a healthy example. Sadly, our friendship never recovered. I tried to always be friendly and supportive, but I had lost my trust and faith in the strength of our old best-friend bond. In retrospect, I do not know what more I could have personally done to prevent our friendship from deteriorating. Perhaps my former best friend, Dawn, was seeking love from that boy in an effort to boost her self-confidence. Perhaps her parents should have intervened and placed more boundaries or limitations on the relationship.

I think perspectives need to be heavily considered in these types of situations. Not understanding where the underlying behaviors are coming from can cause misconceptions. People can never be certain of why people act the way that they do. There are always underlying factors that contribute to the actions and reactions of people, especially preadolescents and teenagers. I feel mental health opportunities are lacking in schools and life in general. Children and adolescents aren't being socialized and taught and modeled how to handle and manage their emotions in productive ways, and when behaviors arise, it seems a punishment is always the answer rather than trying to find out the underlying factor in the behavior and what is really going on in the lives of others. You never know what someone else is going through.

TEX

I witnessed many students take a turn for the worse. We lived in a rural area, which offered little to do in the way of recreation, so many kids fell into risk-taking behaviors very early in their lives—as early as sixth grade. Sadly, many of these kids did end up getting pregnant and dropping out of school or being incarcerated for typical drug and theft charges. It was a low-income area that had few resources. Many parents were experiencing problems of their own with substance abuse and domestic issues, so parental involvement was low and detrimental at best. One friend, we will call him "Tex," was never a great student and probably borderline special needs. Socially, he was popular and well liked by me and the rest of the peers in our small country school. I spent a lot of time with Tex, and my mother was always trying to act like a motherly figure to him since his birth mother was in jail for heroin charges. Tex and I drifted apart during high school because he began smoking marijuana and quickly escalated to harder drugs. His aunt, who had custody of him, was elderly and incapable of knowing the ways of the world today. As a result, Tex basically went untethered through his high school years. Upon graduating, he began to deal in meth and was hospitalized for psychiatric reasons because of an overdose on bath salts. Directly following this incident, Tex was arrested for stealing from a local store. Police found, upon his arrest, a pocketful of crystal meth and away Tex went. I hope that the prison sentence will give him an opportunity to get clean and start fresh upon his release.

PARENTS TO THE RESCUE

A student I had gone to school with from kindergarten through middle school was suddenly unenrolled and homeschooled. Our peer group was shocked and did not understand this very weird transition. He seemed to accept this new homeschooling and really communicated that he was okay with this unorthodox situation. Prior to being homeschooled, his most severe negative behaviors were that he really just acted like a class clown and had the typical middle school behaviors, definitely nothing to warrant being pulled out of a regular school setting. It wasn't long after he began the homeschooling that his parents thought he could still "hang out" with his public school friends. The boy went to prom and all that stuff but just didn't go to a normal school. The boy had been really sheltered-because he was an only child, and then in his high school years, he really broke out and drank all of the time and drove drunk. He experimented with hard drugs. Luckily his parents were totally on top of it and sought help for him. He got into a great college and is doing fantastic now, but it just goes to show you how important the surrounding people can be in a person's life. Without the intervention of the parents, this kid could be in big trouble at this point.

NICK

A behavior problem that I have witnessed with my other peers during my school years is a student being disruptive and belligerent. The other students and I noticed that one particular kid, "Nick," seemed to be having a tough day. Once the teacher tried to talk to Nick to see what might be wrong, the situation escalated immediately. The student started to get an attitude with the teacher and began to belittle the instructor loudly. Before anyone could intervene, Nick got up, gathered his stuff, and walked out of the door. Before exiting the classroom, Nick threw all of his school supplies over the second-floor walkway, leaving them to land in a disheveled heap on the first level (also nearly hitting the janitor, who was mopping the first-level floor). The entire class watched in shock as papers flew everywhere, along with books and everything else. I, along with everyone else, was shocked by what we had just witnessed. Ultimately, the teacher exited our area and followed Nick to the principal's office.

After the incident, Nick started getting therapy that focused on his anger issues. When I saw him once or twice, later that year, he seemed to be much calmer and doing okay in his classes. I definitely think that Nick needed therapy. Getting the help he needed made a major positive difference in his life. The textbook states, "Principals have become reluctant, for example, to suspend youths for acts such as acting insubordinate, wearing outlandish clothing, loitering in halls, and creating classroom disturbances; only a few decades earlier, such conduct would have drawn a quick notice of suspension" (Jette & Killham, 2016). To suspend a student right away is not going to fix the student's behavior; rather, professionals need to figure out why the student did what he or she did and address the problems rather than suspending or expelling the student for outbursts or meltdowns.

SALLY

I met "Sally" when she was only 7 years old. Sally was bright and inquisitive, a girl who excelled in school and loved learning. She was curious and enjoyed exploring how things worked, often dissecting anything she could get her hands on. Unfortunately, when she turned 12, she changed so much that it was like night and day. Sally started back talking to teachers, not doing her homework, and skipping school. Sally even started smoking cigarettes. She began stealing cigarettes or money to buy them. Her behaviors made family life for her parents difficult and stressful. Sally stayed in constant trouble, so much so that her parents were regularly notified of Sally's misbehaviors. Her grades began to drop drastically, and everyone was on high alert as to what could be happening to Sally. "The younger the onset of drug abuse, the greater the negative consequences to the person's cognitive, interpersonal, and education development. There is evidence that children and adolescents are particularly vulnerable to physical problems associated with exposure to alcohol, drugs, and tobacco products" (Jette, 2016). Sally's mother and father almost divorced as a result of the stress and strain Sally's misbehaviors caused in their family life. I noticed a lot of her behaviors began when her father was assigned to the night shift and her mother gave birth to Sally's third sibling. Sally was the eldest child, and with the father working late and long hours, coupled with her mother needing assistance with the younger siblings, Sally just felt left out with all the changes, not to mention the regular stress of puberty and middle school. I felt like the school guidance counselor should have talked to Sally to find out what was going on in her life. The obvious major negative changes should have been warning signs to the teachers and counselor.

JOHNNY

I met "Johnny" when he was 9 years old in our suburban elementary school. Johnny had risky behaviors when I met him, even at that young age. He was a very nice boy, generally, but had a bad temper that could be triggered very quickly and with almost no instigation. He participated on the wrestling team at our school when I first met him, and it became evident that he potentially suffered from emotional control issues. He would cry if he lost a match, almost to the point of total loss of control. I felt that he was extremely hard on himself, especially in a losing situation. While the rest of us would demonstrate disappointment at a loss and just shrug it off with the promise of trying harder next time, Johnny was unable to move past a disappointment. As Johnny grew older, the emotional control issues deteriorated even further. He got worse. Johnny began to exhibit self-destructive behaviors like punching walls and lockers if he lost a match. An extreme and strange incident occurred in our eighth- to ninth-grade years. Johnny encountered a wrestler he was incapable of beating, and instead of moving forward and continuing to wrestle as he had been doing, he chose to avoid the wrestler. To avoid having another match with the particular wrestler, Johnny decided he would drop two weight classes. For those who aren't familiar with wrestling, dropping weight classes is very difficult and not healthy at that age. My peers could not believe how emaciated Johnny had become. After a school/coach investigation, it was found that he took diet pills, withheld food, and exercised like a maniac in hot suits and with the temperature cranked as high as it would go to make himself lose all the weight. My peers and I were surprised mostly by Johnny's parents. They did nothing and were fully aware of this unhealthy situation. His parents turned a blind eye to all the drugs he had been ingesting, until one day they nearly killed him. His mom had to rush him to the hospital, where his stomach was pumped. A passerby had luckily found Johnny unconscious in his bathroom. The only thing that happened as a result of the overdose was that the coach asked him to spend 3 days in the hospital to get evaluated. There was an excuse made by Johnny's mother and father that someone had put drugs in his protein shake.

Johnny's problems continued after graduation resulting in Johnny winding up in jail. Johnny's biological father finally stepped in and took responsibility for his son and asked that the mother and stepfather cease communications with Johnny. Johnny was from a divorced family, and the mom eventually remarried his biological father, who worked long hours and was typically out of town on oil rigs. The parents split again, and the confusion of the marriages, divorces, and remarriages led Johnny to drink a lot of alcohol and smoke marijuana. It was obvious from a young age that Johnny had weak coping skills. As a result, so many things should have happened! The biological father should have paid more attention to what was happening with his son, regardless of the divorce. His child should have come first. The mother and stepdad should have gotten their son a counselor or mental health expert to help when she saw him crying and punching walls over losing matches. You could see this child was hurting inside and angry. In addition, the school should have done something once Johnny almost overdosed. According to a reading from *Real-Life Issues of Tweens and Teens: A Human Development Perspective*, "most adolescent drug abuse prevention programs focus on keeping students from experimenting with tobacco, alcohol, and marijuana, which have been identified as "gateway drugs" (Jette & Killham, 2016).

JIMMY

I met "Jimmy" when he was a baby. When he got older, Jimmy was a great kid who was being led down the wrong path by his peers, in addition to the strain of being in adolescence. He had great parents who loved him dearly, and they did everything for their children. Being such an active child, Jimmy was always kept busy in activities provided by his parents. He was encouraged to play one sport during each season, which he did enthusiastically. His parents had one rule: If he signed up for the sport, he had to play to the completion of the season. It was a team commitment. Jimmy's brother tried some sports alongside his brother but just did not bond with the other kids on the teams as much as Jimmy did.

Jimmy's parents permitted his friends to come over on a regular basis, and his house became a sort of "regular" place where the kids would congregate. Suddenly, after Jimmy's 13th birthday, he began to desire to spend time at places other than his own home. He begged his parents to let him go to a few sleepovers with people they knew. The lies for Jimmy began as "the team is having a pool party," and the parents were going to be home to monitor. Jimmy's mom had an unexpected baby, and with all the attention the baby needed, it became apparent that she lost track of Jimmy—but only in a slight way. Or should I say a lot? Jimmy experimented with drinking, trying marijuana, and having sex with his high school sweetheart, which he always had abstained from prior to middle adolescence. The relationship progressed to the point that Jimmy and his girlfriend were discussing marriage. Jimmy's parents had no idea of the negative route that Jimmy was embracing. Jimmy and his brother got into a major argument that exposed the truth about what Jimmy had been doing. Jimmy sustained a broken nose and black eyes during the fight with his brother regarding his behavior and drug usage.

His brother intervened, perhaps not in the healthiest manner, giving Jimmy an ultimatum. Jimmy's brother reminded him of everything their parents had sacrificed for the family, and he refused to allow Jimmy to ruin the family's reputation because of a girl and drugs. Jimmy's parents took him to see a family member who was having health problems because of drug use. It was a scare tactic, and it must have worked. Thankfully, Jimmy turned his life around; he refuses to do drugs and is working out and is healthier than ever. Jimmy has a solid and healthy relationship with a very nice young lady. I am very glad that the family was able to unite and conquer these negative, downward spiraling behaviors. Perhaps they could have employed the help of a professional counselor or psychiatrist; however, I am still happy that they were able to handle the situation with the help of their family members.

RHODA

M y peer, "Rhoda," had been diagnosed with attention deficit hyperactivity disorder (ADHD) at a young age. She frequently exhibited risk-taking behaviors, especially in the middle school years. There was much consideration by Rhoda regarding the effect of her wild and sometimes dangerous behaviors on her peer group. The impulsivity of the behaviors was literally scary to the peer group and the teachers. These actions were the primary reason that Rhoda was perpetually punished. For example, in eighth grade, Rhoda punted a basketball into the woods during the lunch break. This was problematic because no person was permitted to retrieve the ball, and as a result, everyone's game was immediately over. This resulted in a major physical altercation that caused many students to get in trouble, and Rhoda was suspended. We all felt that she'd punted the ball to get attention or to possibly be malicious because she felt left out. The resulting consequences changed the end of the year for our entire class. While Rhoda was suspended for the last two days of the year, the class celebration was canceled. Rhoda's behavior was certainly looked at as needing improvement. Parents and counselors were involved, and Rhoda eventually switched schools. I hope she is doing well, as I am certain that the constant ADHD impulsive behaviors were problematic in her life and her social life as well.

LOST FATHER

A current close friend of mine was an impulsive, high-energy kid growing up. I was very close to him through school and was there for him when he lost his father in the fifth grade. He was never the same person after the tragedy, and I felt for him. He began to act out at school and impulsively take risks outside of school. At one point, his behavior led him to some strict discipline with his mother, after almost getting kicked out of school for drug and alcohol usage. Not only did he already seem predisposed to at-risk behavior because of his impulsivity but also the additional stress of losing his father just really complicated things exponentially. The step that should have been taken to correct his behavior would have been talking to a counselor, although I think the discipline he went through in football and wrestling shaped his attitude and behavior for the better, more so than that of speaking to a professional would have. I believe that the coaches had a major understanding of what he was going through and took personal, above the required, initiative to help him be successful with his attention-seeking behavior. I believe that the coaches, with their fatherly and male-oriented approach, possibly took some of the edge off of his loss and made all the difference for this friend.

CLOSER TO HOME

This is a recent story about a peer who had troubling behavior throughout high school. We were extremely close because of football and sports. The whole team would always be together, hanging out very often. That was high school, but then it became time to decide on a school for college. My peer decided to attend a branch campus of Ohio State, which was 13 hours away from where the rest of us were located and hours away from our prospective collegiate choices. I think this geographical difference is what sparked his sudden delinquent behaviors. It was not until the winter break that we were all able to visit together. It was at that time that it occurred to our usual peer group that he had become entangled with an unsavory group of peers at the branch campus. His behaviors, including binge drinking, smoking, and trying harder drugs, such as ecstasy and LSD, landed him on academic probation. Because we really cared about him and wanted better for him, we took actions in the manner of talking to him first. It was quickly discovered that he was experiencing homesickness and depression because of his long commute. What he thought would be great for him, getting away and starting anew, did not necessarily work out. At the end of the conversation, he thanked us for opening his eyes to the path he was heading down. Later in the year, he actually decided to transfer back to our hometown and attend the community college while working. He significantly changed his behavior for the betterment of his emotional and mental health, which led to his ultimate success.

JEROME

I can think of many individuals who had issues with behavior during our teenage years, especially middle school. These behaviors ranged from truancy to experimenting with drugs and sex. One of my peers in high school, we will call him "Jerome," experimented with marijuana and pills that he found in his parents' medicine cabinet. This drug usage resulted in excessive lethargy and caused him to miss school. Jerome, in my opinion, chose to exhibit these behaviors publicly in an attempt to fit in with the older group at the high school. I know Jerome desired a shock factor when he was under the influence and felt that he would be considered "hard core" because of his unlimited access to substances that were essentially illegal. I am quite certain that he had low self-esteem and that being accepted by his peers helped him with his self-concept, self-esteem, and feeling more popular and respected by the bad crowd.

Jerome could have been helped with a supportive, personalized relevant learning environment. This type of support would have given Jerome a personal relationship with a teacher or older person who was safe and who would recognize that Jerome was experiencing issues with popularity and solidarity with our cohort rather than simply seeking it with an older, wild crowd. The teacher could have contacted Jerome's parents, and as a team, they could have worked together with Jerome on social skills and building a stronger connection with positive role models (Arnette, 2016, p. 18).

WYATT

M y friend in middle school, whom we will call "Wyatt," enjoyed leaving school and texting the rest of our classmates with pictures throughout the day. In my opinion, Wyatt was pulling these "pranks" in an effort to be funny, but deeper than that was perhaps that he felt left out. While the rest of our class did not necessarily view Wyatt as an outcast, he did make it difficult to truly befriend him. The reason for this is that Wyatt developed a poor reputation because of his stunts, and this made our parents veer away from allowing us to befriend him or hang out with him. This only exacerbated the problem. Wyatt did end up becoming academically challenged because of missing class, and the school resource officer was continually pursuing him throughout the school day. This technically caused Wyatt to become an even bigger outcast: What group of middle school kids wants to be friends with a boy who basically had a resource officer with him all day, every day? The ultimate prank was when Wyatt left school, yet again, and used a high school student's car after stealing the keys. The police were inevitably involved, and the end result was Wyatt being expelled from school.

I believe that if Wyatt had been offered some type of mental health services, perhaps counseling, he could have learned a new skill set regarding relationship building. Also, Wyatt's attention-seeking behavior was at first funny and risky but became routine and literally made us all just "eye roll." It definitely lost its effectiveness, and Wyatt needed to learn healthier ways to get attention and make friends.

CASE

YAVONNE

45

This is about a peer named "YaVonne" from middle school. YaVonne was a girl who had extremely strict parents. This worked well when she was younger, but as she grew older, and still wasn't permitted to do normal things, like dances, sleepovers, or school trips, she began to revolt. This resulted in her attempts to be included. To do so, she began to lie about everything to her parents. When YaVonne did get out from under her parents' thumbs, even for just a short period of time, she had very risk-taking behaviors. YaVonne was like two different people. Sometimes her behaviors were over the top and a bit scary to the rest of us. She had been so controlled for so long, it was as if she never had an opportunity to just be like the rest of us and relax and have a good time. YaVonne developed extreme behaviors and did all the wrong textbook things: drugs, sex, dangerous dares, etc. While her parents attempted to maintain control, they actually pushed her farther to the dark side. YaVonne got pregnant and dropped out of school, which was quite a shame, as she had been an excellent student with many college prospects. I feel that if her parents had let her experience some type of normalcy, she might not have resorted to such extreme measures to experience a typical "kid's life."

SAMANTHA

46

D uring our high school and early college years, a friend I will call "Samantha" demonstrated risk-taking behaviors that were highly unusual when compared to her prior behaviors. She began adolescence as a quiet and happy girl. Samantha had several close friends and excelled in school. Samantha was developmentally ahead of our group of girls and developed a mature female figure long before the rest of us. She had always been friendly and dependable, nothing was ever expected to be abnormal with her personality and behaviors.

Samantha's parents fought constantly while remaining in an unhappy marriage. When Samantha turned 16, she confessed to dealing with periods of depression. Her family circumstances continued to decline, as her mother became permanently disabled. At this time, it seemed as though the familial problems escalated, which in turn forced Samantha to stay away as much as possible. The constant verbal abuse between her parents had broken her spirit. Samantha was in school, worked almost full time, and spent the remainder of her time at the homes of whoever would allow her to stay. She began drinking and spending less time with her friends, isolating herself and falling deeper into depression. In addition, Samantha began using drugs on a regular basis, which resulted in academic problems and getting fired from her job. At that point, Samantha began selling prescription drugs that she stole from her mother.

After much work, Samantha eventually graduated from high school with below-average grades, making her ineligible for scholarships and grants that she had previously aspired to. She was forced to go to a branch college and continue living with her parents, despite having her sights once set on Ivy League schools. Samantha experienced a further downward spiral after beginning college. Her depression was severe at this point, and I later discovered that she had begun cutting herself in addition to continuing her other destructive behaviors. Ultimately, Samantha hit what was her personal rock bottom and began receiving high-level therapy. Samantha currently receives medication, which when coupled with the therapy seems to have really set her back on the path to a healthier, drug-free lifestyle.

OLIVIA

47

"Olivia" was an excellent all-A student who was extremely popular and excelled in extracurricular activities. Her parents were authoritative in style, being as they demonstrated warmth and affection. The family was a stereotypical suburban, middle-class family. Olivia's mother was astay at home parent, and her father was the full-time breadwinner. Olivia and I were best friends and frequented each other's homes every chance we got.

During our eighth-grade year, Olivia's father passed away from a sudden heart attack. This devastating loss was disastrous for the family. I feel immediate counseling should have taken place, as the grieving process was so severe for Olivia, her sibling, and her mother. This simple step could have changed the course of Olivia's life. Obviously, after the death of the father, Olivia's mother had to take a job to fulfill the financial household obligations. This left Olivia with little to no supervision, all while struggling with grief and loneliness. Olivia began to distance herself from her typical peer group and began to act moody, erratic, and often negative or unpleasant in general. Although I struggled to remain friends with Olivia for several years after he father's passing, it was not an easy friendship to maintain, nor was it healthy. Olivia was regularly angry and vicious toward people. Her continued negativity really caused a rift in our relationship that could not be repaired.

DARIUS

Darius was a young man with musical talent and an extremely bright future. He was the youngest of three children, and his parents both worked full-time lucrative jobs Although Darius was never an honor-roll student, he got by with passing grades. Darius was tasked with assisting with the care of his older sister, who suffered from cerebral palsy. During middle school and high school, Darius was a star in the band, of which his older brother was a member. They frequently spent time together in their home practicing, composing, and recording themselves.

It was through this experience that Darius formed a band not affiliated with the school. These bandmates and Darius began experimenting with drugs and alcohol. Darius's grades fell further into a desperate situation. Darius spent less time with positive peer groups and the school band, and more time with the older bandmates who were not proving to be good influences. His parents made numerous attempts to discipline him by "breaking up" the band and forbidding him to hang out with the band-mates, but they had little success. Already, so much of the parental time and energy was spent on their sick daughter that the boys were often left to their own devices. The lack of support and supervision, by no fault of the parents, led Darius, and perhaps his brother, to make bad choices. Even from an early age, the brothers took unnecessary risks, such as playing on railroad tracks and riding in cars with people who had been drinking and smoking marijuana.

At 15, Darius and his brother were in a car wreck with a friend who was under the influence of drugs and alcohol. Fortunately, both survived; however, this incident was not taken with the seriousness it deserved. If Darius and his brother had been able to latch on to a better peer group and had adults who intervened at this point, they probably would not have continued this behavior and bonded in healthier ways with more positive people, or perhaps the school band, again. Unfortunately, it continued through high school. Thankfully, Darius and his brother were able to rise above the negative experiences and go to college. They are both now married with children and living a healthy life as was intended.

JARED

CASE

49

Change is an inevitable and healthy part of life and development. This can be part of emotional, social, or physical change, or a combination of all aspects of development. Sadly, it's common for such changes to occur in many children and teens that end in negative outcomes. Unfortunately, many of us are not strangers to knowing people who have undergone such negative changes, and it can result in tragic events. Throughout my life, I have witnessed these occurrences too many times and in varying degrees: losing friends, trying to help only to be denied, or general energy spent helping people in a downward spiral.

The first peer, "Jared," is one that I remember clearly. The most harrowing incident occurred in the second-fourth grade. It was the first day of school when I first met Jared. He was new and rode my school bus. We became fast friends. All the typical things transpired as they do with new friends. It was only a few months before my other longtime friends began to express concerns. This was confusing to me, and I wondered if there was jealousy. My longtime friends explained that Jared was acting mean and aggressive toward them, that Jared intimidated them, and that they did not understand why we were friends. I initially disregarded their concerns and figured it was definitely jealousy. I mean, I had not seen any of this bullying whatsoever. I hadn't a clue as to why Jared and my longtime friends hadn't bonded as well as we had. As time passed and I became acquainted with Jared more during the school year, I gradually began to recognize exactly what my friends were claiming; he would verbally abuse my longtime friends by speaking vulgar statements to them. The longtime friends were already not friendly with each other, but the repetitive verbal taunting made me recognize this disturbing behavior as alarming and scary. It escalated to the point that I was fearful of being around Jared, even though he had never bullied me or expressed any aggression toward me. His behavior gradually escalated, and he was continually punished by the teachers. None of the punishments or lectures seemed to deter these aggressions, and eventually, Jared was expelled from school when he had an outburst that included him saying, "I'm bringing my gun to school, and I'm going to blow all of your heads off." Obviously, this warranted much involvement from teachers, law enforcement, administrators, and his parents. As a result, he was removed from the school and sent to an institution that focused primarily on behavioral problems in young adolescents. Sadly, I have not seen or heard from him since.

JANE

I will refer to a peer who experienced problems as "Jane." I met Jane the first day of high school, and we quickly became friends because of similar interests. Freshman year flew by, and Jane and I were great friends and were together every moment possible. Jane was a very studious student and really placed the utmost priority on her schoolwork. Sophomore year arrived, and once more, we were in class together, which resulted in further friendship bonding. At the end of sophomore year, however, I recall her confiding in me about new "friends" she had met at the library. She divulged that her new friends were wild and doing things such as parties, drinking, and drugs. During junior year, I gradually started seeing Jane less because she was constantly hanging with the "library" friends instead of me. When we did visit with each other, her stories primarily focused on their drinking and weed-smoking stories, with many stories ending in who was having sexual escapades with whom. I would harp on her, repeatedly tell her that she should not be doing any of that stuff because it was bad for her. "Blah blah blah" was the typical response I received. I revealed that I was worried about her and felt like I was watching her slide down a slippery slope. Of course, all this resulted in was Jane further ignoring me and me continuing to "harp."

Jane began skipping school rather frequently, which was shocking considering her prior concern for perfect grades. I would constantly express my concern about her, which she would disregard and try to assure me that she was "fine." Her behavior, unfortunately, continued to decline, until it was so bad that Jane did not return for our senior year. I've kept in touch through the years since, and she had told me that because of all the bad things she was doing, eventually everything imploded, and as a result, Jane chose to withdrawal from school for a year in order to attend rehab and get the help she needed that I could not provide.

JAMES

I will call a peer of mine who was doing risk-taking behaviors "James." James had been a good friend of mine since sixth grade. He was a very genuine person and one of the sweetest people I have ever met. Fast-forward to our junior year of high school and everything was going great for both of us. We were never in trouble and basically straight-edge kids who didn't do anything we weren't allowed to do. One weekend, James, another friend of ours, and I had decided to go a bit wild and spend a night together drinking. Everything went fine. We all drank within moderation and didn't actually end up going wild. Thinking back, James was definitely the most inebriated, but we all enjoyed ourselves and didn't think too much about it. One thing that stuck in my mind were the days following our drinking event. I had noticed a little change in James. He became much more focused on when we could drink together again, so much so that he would recommend it every week, even after the other friend and I had voted against it time and time again. During the times that we denied the drinking party request, James would get angry and claim we didn't like him anymore. My friend and I began to grow very worried about James because of his obsession with drinking opportunities, and we later found out that since we wouldn't partake with him, he would just drink by himself in his room. That was the tipping point for us. My friend and I approached him soon afterward, and we expressed our concerns about him and how his unhealthy habit would surely ruin him if he continued. Luckily, our words resonated with him, and James quickly gave up the drinking because he didn't want to worry us. We were very glad we were able to curb his behavior before it got out of hand.

People are constantly changing throughout their lives. Many of the changes occur because of new interactions and experiences. Sometimes, the changes aren't always for the better; they can run amok within a person. Over my years, I've been no stranger to such occurrences in my friends. I have seen it to different degrees throughout my friend group, and sadly because of such changes, some people are no longer my friends. It is something that you have to be careful about. Changing in ways that can be harmful to you and others should be avoided, because there is no worse feeling than losing friends to bad habits/behaviors.

SARAH

In middle school, my friend "Sarah" was known for her risk-taking choices and promiscuous behavior. Sarah was closer to her mother because her father was an alcoholic. This was likely a reason for her parents' divorce. Sarah was always seeking love from men, and this resulted in a constant cycle of abusive relationships. Recently, she became involved with an older man, Ryan, who was known for his excessive drinking and smoking marijuana. Although I expressed my concerns, Sarah started slowly adopting Ryan's choices into her own lifestyle. I felt her parents could have been more expressive about her decisions, but I don't think they fully understood the level of her involvement with these newfound choices. In addition, her teachers noticed her grades and participation slipping, but again, I don't think anyone had complete awareness of her actions.

Sarah began consistently skipping school, disconnecting completely from friends and family, and spent all of her time with Ryan. By the end of eighth grade, Sarah became pregnant. Looking back, I am sure that everyone in Sarah's life could have been more vocal in expressing opinions, trying to help her change, and addressing their concerns about Ryan; however, I feel the real concerns were Sarah's lack of a strong male figure in her life, her parents' abusive relationship, and her unhealthy home life. Currently, Sarah is seeking her GED and taking care of her baby as a single mother.

ANDREW

In high school, my classmate, "Andrew," had a plethora of behavior problems. Andrew constantly skipped school, smoked marijuana, took drugs,
and had little care for much in life. Andrew's friends all shared his mentality
of a carefree lifestyle that revolved around drugs, alcohol, and delinquent
behavior. Andrew's parents appeared detached and uninvolved in his life.
However, fortunately, we had an amazing math teacher, Mrs. Smith, who
cared deeply for her students and their futures.

Mrs. Smith was exceptionally different from all other faculty members.
She strived to have an impact on all of her students, often going out of her
way to ensure that they excelled. Her diligence in trying to change Andrew's
life allowed him to see her as a positive role model. Over time, she remained
close with Andrew through graduation. Quite honestly, I don't think he
would have made it without her. In fact, at our graduation ceremony, Mrs.
Smith was there cheering for him as he received his diploma.

KATY

During high school, my classmate "Katy" was rude and disrespectful to teachers, faculty members, and other peers. She was constantly late to class and had accumulated enough absences that she was close to being expelled. Every quarter, the principal would call her to his office to discuss a plan for reducing her absences, although it never seemed to work. Fortunately, she was able to maintain decent grades from her sheer intelligence, which kept the principal at bay, at least for a while. Although her behavior was less delinquent than other classmates, the reason for her behavior choices was perhaps the most concerning of all. Katy was severely depressed and addicted to drugs as a result of her parents' recent divorce. She masked her pain with humor and acted aloof about the situation. It was challenging to know her because few people were fully aware of her home life and the hardships she faced every day after school. Her parents were the clear choice in helping her, but they were the cause of her pain and were too consumed in their own problems to even notice her issues. Our teachers knew something was wrong, but because Katy kept her grades high and was attentive in class, they didn't ask questions. Also, teachers definitely knew something was up, but she was a quiet-enough student and did well enough that nobody really took the time to ask her what was going on. Eventually, Katy began to struggle through school and barely made it to graduation because of her absences and lack of effort. She and I are no longer acquaintances since graduation, as she decided to take time off rather than go to college. To my knowledge, she is still struggling with the same issues, and her parents' divorce continues to dictate her choices.

AUSTIN

As a 6-year-old, I remember my 13-year old neighbor "Austin" was known as the local bully. Austin and his group of friends were notorious for vandalizing property, beating up younger children, being rude to adults, stealing alcohol, and skipping school. Unfortunately, I was one of Austin's most favorite kids to pick on. It's painful to relive, but I can remember all the fights I lost to his gang and how they would torture me. Furthermore, Austin would do little things to aggravate my life. For instance, he would climb up the large tree in my yard to nail or tie up my belongings, such as my bike, action figures, bike wheels, or favorite toys. Austin was the epitome of a typical bully from the movies with all the same behaviors. Austin's younger brother Brian and I were good friends. This enabled me to see the opposite side of their life in an abusive household with a drunk dad. Occasionally, Austin would show empathy toward me, but that was rare. I think that bullying made him feel powerful and in control, and that it was an expression of his deep pain.

When I was 9, my parents divorced, and I moved to Ohio with my mom. Now I am 25 years old and recently found out that Austin is in jail for rape and robbery. Thinking back, I should have told my parents about the bullying. Their involvement might have curbed his behavior, because I know Austin was a decent human being and just needed help from someone. My hope now is that jail can be the catalyst he needs to change.

CODY

A peer of mine, "Cody," was a bit of a nerd and loner, and quiet. However, when approached, Cody was pleasant, kind, and responsive. Cody and I rode the bus every day, and over time, we had enough interactions that we slowly became friends. Cody was an excellent student and expressed his interest in pursuing nursing in college. One day, Cody expressed that he had feelings for me. Although I had no idea, I began texting him outside of school to see if any interest was present. Things were going well, but randomly, Cody messaged me that he was very depressed, felt life was not worth living, and had numerous thoughts about ending his life. I took this as both a sign and a desperate plea for help. Immediately, I called the police and met the officers at a local river where Cody often visited. When we found Cody, he agreed to go with the police to the hospital and asked that I go too, until his parents came. Once his mother arrived, I spoke with her privately, expressing that I would inform her immediately should Cody ever express any signs of this behavior or mind-set again. On one other occasion, Cody informed me of his depression and noted that his poor home life as the cause. As promised, I immediately informed his mother. After that day, I never heard from Cody again and always wondered if I helped or harmed his situation.

Several years have passed, and sporadically Cody has popped up as a mutual Facebook friend. I learned that he became a nurse, got married, and had children, and he happily smiled in all his pictures. This was the most rewarding discovery because I felt hopeful that my decision to intercede was the reason for his change of course. In that moment, I knew I had done the right thing and would go on to encourage others to help those in need as well.

NATE

M y high school classmate, "Nate," was constantly disruptive and disrespectful, and he always skipping school. He was notorious for fighting with peers, being in detention, and failing classes. I found out through mutual friends that his mood swings were a result of street drugs. He fought with many of the students. He was into taking pills and skipped school a lot. Unsurprisingly, he did poorly in school and was close to being expelled; it appeared unlikely that he would graduate. However, he portrayed his tough attitude and cool demeanor as if they were his saving grace.

Nate was an only child, and I later found out that his parents were very absent in his life. In fact, starting when Nate was in elementary school, they would either pass him off to others or leave him home alone on most occasions. I was told that Nate was actually a sweet, kind, and considerate person who excelled in school. However, with time, Nate changed his mannerisms as his parents grew more preoccupied, leaving him more isolated. Coincidently, Nate started getting picked on by older students in junior high school and had no role models or help to aid him with this significant problem. Apparently, Nate felt the only way to deal with the situation was to make poor choices and self-medicate, which led to his downfall. Nate never graduated, but once he moved out of his parents' house, he received his GED.

JEREMY

CASE

58

My peer, "Jeremy," was our class nerd. Almost all schools have different cliques or groups, but, unfortunately, Jeremy didn't fit into any of them. He sat by himself on the bus, at lunch, in classes, and during gym. He was such a loner that he was almost invisible to others. I would go out of my way to try and speak with him, and initiate conversation. However, I think Jeremy felt so alone that he never tried to spark a conversation with me. This continued until high school when Jeremy showed up the first day of freshmen year looking very different. He portrayed himself as a "jock," wearing all the latest trends. At first, the only reaction he received was judgment, gossip, and speculation. However, amazingly, over time, Jeremy started to hang out with the popular group of peers. He would tell jokes, talk to everyone, act silly in class, and even made tryouts for the football team. As time progressed, Jeremy's instant fame started to dwindle, and people stopped caring about him again. Once again, Jeremy was invisible. He'd put so much effort into trying that this was devastating for him. This setback led to his involvement with the wrong crowd, who skipped school, took drugs, drank alcohol, and had no future ambitions. By graduation, Jeremy had been suspended so many times that he couldn't graduate. Sometime after high school, I heard that he did obtain a GED, but he was still involved in a similar crowd in my hometown, working at a Home Depot, and selling drugs.

AARON

CASE

59

During high school, my close friend "Aaron" constantly struggled with authority and rules. Aaron and I met on our school swim team and became close, even though he was two grades ahead of me. I enjoyed hanging out with Aaron during swim practice, but in school, we were never close. I noticed that he was constantly confrontational with teachers, arguing just because he had been instructed to do something. He eventually started smoking and drinking. He skipped practices and had poor performance. Our coach kicked him off the team. This further led to Aaron's disregard of authority and a lack of commitment to school. Oddly, Aaron had a good life with caring parents and a happy home. Although he was the oldest child, his four younger siblings appeared to get more attention than he did. I always felt this contributed to his behavioral issues because he just wanted attention. After his split from the swim team, I lost touch with, and interest in, Aaron. I heard that he struggled in college, eventually dropped out, and was working as a landscaper. I am not sure if he actually continued with drugs and alcohol, but I know he continued to hang out with a crowd that did.

JORDAN

My longtime peer, "Jordan," was one of my best friends throughout our academic careers. In high school, we took all the same classes. So we would spend most nights and weekends hanging out and working on homework. Jordan was highly intelligent and passed all of his courses without much effort. In general, he kept mostly to himself and was relatively well behaved in high school. However, once Jordan got into college, he became primarily concerned with extending his social network and joined a fraternity. Jordan's mind-set from high school of not needing to apply himself carried over to college, and it slowly affected his grades and life choices. He skipped most of his classes, and his GPA became so low, he was teetering on being kicked out of school. Unfortunately, this pattern continued, and Jordan went from a smart student with a bright future to a college dropout. Fortunately for Jordan, this may have been the best solution because he moved home, began working nights and weekends, and saved enough money to start a small company. This is a rare case of a problem becoming a blessing, but also an inspirational story that any person can change, regardless of their circumstances.

LUKE

It was always enlightening to be in class with "Luke!" He was so intelligent that half the time he ended up educating our teachers about a class topic. Luke would push all our teachers to further prepare for class, making them ready for all his questions. To his peers and his teachers, he was a very gifted individual. In particular, physics class was the best because Luke was a modern-day Einstein. However, the boys in homeroom would tease, torture, and ridicule Luke. Although they constantly called him names and taunted him, Luke mostly ignored them until his cousin started at our school. Luke wanted to appear cool and tough in front of his family, and immediately he started to change his behavior. In classes, Luke would be rude to teachers and peers, and overly inappropriate. He started skipping classes, not completing homework, and taking drugs. The boys who ridiculed him were still persistent in wanting to expose his true self, so one day, they gave him an ultimatum. They said Luke needed to smoke crack or else they would beat him up after school. His cousin perceived him as cool, so he kept encouraging Luke to just smoke it. After Luke smoked crack, the boys kept pushing ultimatums on him every day that resulted in fighting if they disagreed. Eventually, Luke started taking drugs and drinking regularly from all the external pressures and lack of escape. His grades and attendance dropped, and Luke started failing out of school. Mrs. Smith, our school psychologist, stepped in and started seeing Luke three times a week. Fortunately, she was able to get Luke back on track enough to graduate. I later found out that Luke attended community college, graduated with honors, and is working in finance. Mrs. Smith was absolutely his savior.

MATT

Mrs. Jones, my eighth-grade geography teacher, was always giving us lots of class projects. In fact, she gave us a project on almost all our class topics. My classmate, "Matt," was always struggling to turn in projects. To make matters worse, Matt always had an excuse for why his project was late or never turned in at all. Rather than allow another excuse, Mrs. Jones decided to add an incentive to one of the projects. Secretly, this idea was to encourage Matt to turn his project in on time, but also to add fun to all our numerous projects. Matt had completed the project and was eager to turn it in; however, his mother put the project folder in his sister's bag that she ended up taking to school across town. Afraid of giving Mrs. Jones another excuse, Matt decided to call in sick to school by pretending to be his mother on the phone. The school then called his mother's work to follow up, and obviously, she became aware of Matt's behavior. Matt was then suspended for lying and grounded by his parents. Matt missed so much school, and his grades were so low, that he had to retake the class the following year. This set Matt back for a late graduation, and he finished with the class below him.

TJ

L iving in a small community, almost everyone knows your business. My friend "TJ" had a very strict and proud father. As kids, we all played and had fun, while TJ had to work in the family bakery seven days a week. TJ's father had him on a strict schedule and didn't allow him to go out often, and when he did, he had an early curfew.

On different occasions, TJ would sneak out at night to hang out with friends, have fun, and get into minor trouble. One night, TJ's dad caught him sneaking out and gave him a beating in front of his friends. His friends were aware that his dad was abusive, aggressive, and used tactics like whipping or the belt as a form of discipline. This incident made TJ become incredibly embarrassed and much quieter in class. However, one day in class, a peer sitting behind TJ made an obscene and rude noise in class. Our teacher, Mr. Morgan, didn't know who made the noise but rather the vicinity in which it arose. He went to TJ and asked if it was him, but he was rather quiet and didn't respond after being asked several times. The teacher grew louder in TJ's face as he asked the same question. Rather than answering, TJ impulsively reacted by smacking the teacher across the face. The teacher, in shock at what had transpired, pointed to the door, and said, "Get out!" TJ, also in shock at what had happened, picked up his books and left the classroom. The principal called TJ's father and suspended him. I can only imagine the beating that TJ received that night from his father.

Once he returned to school, TJ was required to see the school psychologist three times a week. Personally, I feel there was blame on both sides, but I also felt that TJ had a lot of home issues that sparked his behavior. Once the school psychologist became involved, TJ's dad was asked to get help. I know that things changed over time as both he and his dad grew older. However, I don't think TJ's life changed until he moved out at 18 years old. I found out that TJ went to a college across the country and hardly ever goes home.

ADAM

In junior high school, my classmate "Adam" was always the class clown. He felt it was funny to bully and poke fun at others, even teachers. He skipped classes, missed school, didn't turn in homework, and disrupted classes. I felt bad for our teachers because they tried so hard to be patient with him, but he thought it was hilarious and amusing to misbehave. Detentions never seemed to work. In high school, I remember him in more of my classes. As we got older, his behaviors seemed to get worse. He was very erratic and loved to talk over others. He would often get in trouble for cursing in class and sometimes at teachers. He was always misbehaving and being sent to the principal's office for detention or suspension.

After high school, Adam was involved in a head-on car crash that took his life. The passenger survived. Unfortunately, the first thought that came to my mind was how unsurprised I was that Adam wasn't wearing a seatbelt because he had always lived his life so carelessly and recklessly. It also made me so sad to think that the mistake cost him his life and how it could have changed.

MICHAEL AND MASON

" Michael" and "Mason" were very close friends in high school. These two were literally inseparable. They rode to school together, ate lunch together, and hung out on nights and weekends. Michael was highly intelligent, but Mason was not as smart. Unfortunately, they started getting into drugs and alcohol together as well. Prior to this, Michael was set to apply to top Ivy League universities; however, over time, his grades and GPA began to fall. Furthermore, they both began skipping so many classes that they each were suspended several times, which caused them to not graduate with our class. In fact, they both had to take retake their senior year. The following year, they barely finished high school. I heard Michael and Mason went to a community college but dropped out. Last I heard, both boys were working as landscape developers for a local company in town.

COUSIN SARAH

M y cousin "Sarah" and I attended the same high school and were also in the same grade. However, we lived two very different lives. We did not share the same last name, so people rarely connected us as being related. Even more than that, we never hung out together. Sarah frequently ran with the group of girls who partied, drank alcohol, and were promiscuous with boys. That group was notorious for slacking in school, showing up late or not at all, making out in bathrooms, and sleeping around on weekends. Sarah was on the verge of failing freshmen year and seemed not to care. Sarah and I were not close, but I found out that she was badly raped over the summer at a concert.

After this, it was apparent that Sarah fell into a deep depression. Before Christmas that year, Sarah committed suicide in her bathroom. The autopsy showed that she had overdosed on her mothers' painkillers, and police found several bottles in her drawers. Sarah's parents were divorced and not great role models, but her death created a huge void in our entire family. Sarah has been gone for over eight years, and it still greatly affects all of us. It's easy to think that a more nurturing and supportive home life might have changed her outcome, but one can only guess. However, her situation constantly makes me evaluate my own progress in life and helps me to maintain a desire to stay on a good and stable path.

BRIAN

During school, I was on an individualized education plan plan, which is designed to help struggling students with a course of action for consistent progress. However, a lot of the students were also class clowns, bullies, and delinquents because they needed a way to rebel against feeling less valued than their peers. In particular, I remember one instance when all the IEP students being tutored after school decided to prank the new substitute teacher. Although I don't remember the exact details, I believe the students expressed something to the degree that they struggle in school because they all live in a local trailer park, have little food, and parents who take drugs and are completely uninvolved. The following day, our primary teacher found out and gave everyone involved detention. This particular group of IEP students was constantly being sent to detention for misbehaving in similar ways.

A different incident involved "Brian," another IEP student who likely had some mental instabilities along with his behavior issues. One particular day, Brian appeared to be having a hard time, and our primary IEP teacher approached him in class to try to talk about his issue. Slowly, Brian started growing more frustrated with our teacher as she probed him with questions. Suddenly, Brian stood up, took his books, walked out the door, and threw all his school supplies over the second-floor walkway. Our whole IEP group watched as papers, pens, pencils, crayons, markers, notebooks, and textbooks flew everywhere, and then slowly began to fall down to the first floor. Everyone was in complete shock that any person could treat a teacher that way, create a scene, and act as though nothing happened. He was immediately sent to the principal's office and suspended.

To close, both situations were very different, yet I noticed a very similar problem. The first resulted in numerous detentions and the other suspension. However, I think it's more important to try to understand the underlying problem(s) with each student rather than just punish them in isolation. The teenage years are a critical time of development with heightened states of emotional instability and irrational, impulsive choices. Educators, counselors, psychologists, parents, and tutors can all become critical saviors in any one person's life, but issues must be understood to be noticed and changed.

KEVIN

My classmate, "Kevin," had become a particularly rowdy and aggressive person. Growing up, he was docile and easygoing, but once his parents divorced, and he was court ordered to live full time with his dad, his behavior quickly changed. Slowly, Kevin became less responsible with his schoolwork and stopped preparing for classes. He would have likely skipped school, but his dad was very strict. Kevin's behavioral changes became evident in school on a day when we had a substitute teacher. This teacher began challenging Kevin all class period on various questions about the course content. Since Kevin did not do the homework, he quickly grew very angry and felt ambushed. After nearly 20 minutes of back and forth arguing, Kevin stood up, spoke unspeakable curse words to the teacher, and stormed out of class. He was immediately sent to the principal's office and suspended. However, once Kevin returned to school, he was required to meet with the school psychologist once a week to understand his issues for the remainder of the year. Furthermore, rather than growing angry, his dad started seeing a therapist with Kevin after school, twice a week.

Over time, Kevin really sorted through is problems both individually and with his dad, and by the start of the next school year, he was back to his easygoing, docile nature. It was very inspirational to witness.

SHARMAINE

My classmate, "Sharmaine," was 16 years old at the start time of this incident. At the time, she lived in an apartment with her mother and two younger siblings. Although she was a different race than me, I would describe Sharmaine as a girl who used her good looks to enhance her promiscuous and aggressive behaviors. During our high school years, she was thin, tall, and had large breasts. She would always wear revealing clothing, such as short skirts and low-cut blouses. She gained a reputation for being easy to obtain sex from, and, obviously, all the guys wanted to sleep with her. However, things changed once we got to junior year, and Sharmaine became pregnant. Sharmaine finished junior year and had her baby at 18 years old. The father wanted nothing to do with her or the baby, and her single mother simply couldn't afford to help her. Sharmaine was forced to drop out of high school and began living on friends' couches until, eventually, she was living in various homeless shelters throughout the city. To make money, Sharmaine would prostitute so she could pay for diapers, wipes, and food. Because of her prostitution, Sharmaine began to use drugs, and soon she contracted HIV, which quickly turned to AIDS. At 19 years old, Sharmaine couldn't afford to obtain health-care treatments for her illness, and she passed away before her 20th birthday. Since her death, her mother has gained full custody of her child.

NATE

My 12-year-old friend named "Nate" lived with his mother, father, and two sisters. Nate, even at a young age, was always trying to fit in with the athletes. Nate's father was a truck driver and was only home on weekends, which left Nate surrounded by women: his mother and sisters. I feel strongly that this contributed to Nate's early onset needs for guy friends and guy sports. Unfortunately, Nate wore glasses and had braces that required him to wear headgear during the day, which resulted in him being heavily bullied at school. After a few years, once Nate finished with braces, a few of the players on the basketball team appeared to befriend him; however, they were just abusing his desperate desire for friends and sportsmanship to bully him into taking drugs. Although Nate's dad was always on the road and relatively absent in his personal life, Nate wanted his dad's advice and waited to talk to him before succumbing to the bas-ketball players' offer. To me, this was God interceding, because after this incident, Nate's dad took the moment very seriously and changed his work schedule so he could be home every night with his family. His dad slowly became more involved in his children's lives, and Nate never felt a need to join sports or feel forced to make guy friends. In fact, Nate and his dad became best friends, and he helped Nate uncover his dream of becoming a lawyer. Today, Nate and I are best friends, and he is currently pursuing that dream. His mother, father, and sisters frequently visit him on campus. Nate and his dad are still the best of friends, and Nate's circle of friends remains very small.

SAM

My friend "Sam" is an only child, lived in a two-bedroom apartment with her single mom in an average part of town, and was 15 years old at the start of her downfall. Unfortunately, Sam and her mother did not have a close relationship, and this division only enhanced Sam's rebellious choices and behavior. At 16 years old, Sam was regularly smoking marijuana, having unprotected sex, and had at least two abortions. Sam's mother worked two jobs and was completely unaware of her lifestyle, friends, or lack of commitment to school. After several incidences, the principal finally reached Sam's mother and informed her of Sam skipping school, her failing grades, smoking marijuana, and hanging with delinquent teenagers, which enraged her mother. This led to a huge argument, which caused Sam to avoid all contact with her mother and move into her friend's basement. Sam's poor behavior choices continued, which resulted in her being arrested for drug possession and court ordered to enter rehab, which was not successful after three attempts. She refused to follow through with treatment, dropped out of high school, and moved to California with an old friend. To my knowledge, Sam never finished high school and is currently a drug dealer out near Long Beach, California. However, I have heard that she is doing relatively well financially, although I imagine her lifestyle won't continue to go well in the long run.

JACOB

Beginning in middle school, one of my peers, "Jacob," started making delinquent choices that eventually led to a lifetime of hardships and struggles. At the start of our freshmen year, only a few weeks into the school year, Jacob got into a serious fight that put two classmates in the hospital, which caused him to be suspended and taken to court by both families. Jacob loved fights, and outside of school, always started them with any passerby. During school, he avoided fistfights but would express his anger with random outbursts at other students, teachers, and faculty members. Jacob grew up in a poor family with an absent father and a mother who always worked, and he could not afford a lifestyle to socially fit in with any group. To combat this issue, Jacob decided to become his own group, and he chose violence, threats, and bullying as his trademark. All of these issues continued through high school. Jacob barely survived high school, but somehow made it to graduation with an extremely low GPA. He never attended college but was encouraged by teachers to attend a trade school, which he did for a while. Later, I found out that he never finished trade school and instead was in jail. After looking him up online, I found out that he had been charged with three counts of homicide. When I saw his mugshot, I noticed that he had a few face tattoos and looked much older than anyone our age. In that moment, I couldn't help but wonder if his life could have possibly gone in a different direction if he'd had a good support system.

JENNA

A girl I grew up with, "Jenna," was horrible at handling challenging situations. She did not know how to handle the bad things that had happened in her youth and held on to them for a long time. Jenna dealt with a lot of bullying because she dressed differently than most and felt a need to express herself despite the bullying. This lack of acceptance from peers promoted deep insecurities and a desperate need for love. Jenna found this love and acceptance in bad relationships, and she became pregnant by sophomore year of high school. Not knowing how to handle it, Jenna immediately got an abortion and then couldn't handle that she'd had an abortion. To cope, Jenna started hanging around drug addicts, became addicted, and then couldn't cope with her new addictions in addition to her abortion. She was using for almost 3 years until she was forced into rehab by her grandmother, who sent her across the country to a facility. Jenna spent 9 months in rehab and returned home a different person. She met with a church counselor once a week, worked at a local nursing home, and volunteered at the soup kitchen once a month. Jenna now has a new boyfriend who gives her the comfort that she needed throughout her childhood and is helping her forgive the past. She always wanted to feel accepted and understood, which she has found in herself and her relationship.

DANIEL

A friend of mine, "Daniel," from middle school was not a bad kid, but he always made bad decisions. Often, he skipped school, never did his homework, and got suspended a few times for cussing out other students and being rude to our teachers during class. He did not get much attention at home, which led to him to get attention in school by misbehaving. Often, he skipped school because his mom didn't care if he went, and a lot of his friends skipped school. During senior year, our homeroom teacher caught him with marijuana, and he was suspended for over a month right before graduation. This caused Daniel's grades to drop so low that he couldn't graduate, which sent him into a deep depression. Without a high school degree, he felt like a failure at life. Before high school, Daniel was always a happy, approachable, smart, friendly, and kind person who dressed well and cared about his overall presentation. Since high school, I learned that Daniel works at a local factory and lives in low-income housing with the same bad group of friends from high school. I think with better support, educators, or guidance counselors, Daniel's life may have ended up entirely different.

PAUL

M y peer "Paul" would always say the worst comments at the worst times. He never tried to filter his words, and it would disturb everyone in the class. Paul never cared about the consequences because his primary objective was to get attention. He would insult teachers, other students, himself, or the topics we discussed in class. Starting as early as eighth-grade, teachers would be forced to take Paul into the hallway to pull him away from other students to make the comments stop. Paul only saw this as funny and would use it to aid in his tormenting and ridicule. This further enhanced the reaction he wanted from peers. Paul didn't care about the punishment because the reaction outweighed the consequences. If another student would say something back to him in a negative way, such as telling him he wasn't funny, or that he needed to be quiet, Paul would make a scene by yelling at him or her. He would cuss the student out and yell degrading things all because the student didn't find his behavior funny. Paul never changed throughout high school and slowly lost all of his friends' respect, and by senior year, no one even looked in his direction. Most of our graduating class went on to college, but Paul ended up working at a local fast-food restaurant. Paul was a relatively bright student in grade school and could have easily gone to college with more guidance.

ROBIN

76

" Robin" was a girl who would always have major violent temper problems, even during class. As soon as she didn't get her way, or someone said something rude to her, she would begin screaming at a high volume and smack whatever items were close by. Robin also would throw everybody's things off of their desks and push over chairs and furniture. Sometimes, she would hit people with items during the throwing rages. She wouldn't always hit people intentionally, which was a relief. The scenes she created were scary and embarrassing and abnormal, considering that the smallest issue would set Robin "off." We (her classmates) could always tell when a major tantrum was looming because she would exhibit repeat behaviors that included tightly clenching her fists and scrunching up her face into a scowl. Some occasions led to the older teachers recognizing these warning signs and de-escalating her by speaking quietly and giving her space. However, the majority of the times when her fists were clenched resulted in violent outbursts that left the classroom looking like a tornado had hit it. Robin would always be punished or receive disciplinary action, such as getting sent to the office or in-school suspension, yet these did not have lasting effects. It was as if she was so angry, she was not in control of herself. She accepted the punishments, but not without being upset. I feel that Robin had some deep psychological problems that needed to be dealt with on a much more professional level instead of her being suspended and being issued demerits.

CHRIS

77

I went to school with a boy named "Chris" who was abusive and continually lied. Chris began hitting other students at a really young age, which appeared very abnormal. Chris automatically struck other children and caregivers when they would attempt to take a toy or something else away from him. By the time he was in the elementary grades, those behaviors occurred on a daily basis, multiple times each day. Chris was constantly punished with time-outs and isolation tactics for the hitting and violent offenses. In addition, he would lie about the transgressions and receive extra punishment as a result. The consequences did not work, as the behaviors never ceased and sometimes worsened. It directly affected his peers because they (we) were the victims in his violent hitting attacks. Because Chris first began exhibiting violent behaviors at a young age, it led to major disturbances in his relationships with his peers. Chris should have been seeing a counselor or professional, as there appeared to be real issues that needed attention rather than punishment. I didn't realize this at the time, because I was so young, but if my own child were to out like Chris, I would immediately deal with it by using mental health professionals and a pediatrician.

LIZ

From as early as middle school, all the way through high school, I knew a girl who I will call "Liz." Liz was extremely bright, but also kind of odd. During grade school, Liz was a class clown, but rarely acted out or caused major behavior problems. In high school, Liz began to make choices that were questionable and appeared to be risky to our peer group. Liz began to try drugs, not hard drugs, but still illegal drugs, such as marijuana. As a result, she began to slack off on her schoolwork, and her grades immediately began to drop from As to Cs. Most disturbing, Liz began to act like a prostitute: using sexual favors to get drugs instead of money. Liz acted out sexually and engaged in provocative behaviors with practical strangers. She would use sexual favors to obtain marijuana at first and then graduated to cocaine. Once Liz entered college, she came out as a lesbian and then later as nonbinary. I believe that if Liz had gone to school in an environment that was less judgmental, she would not have channeled the frustration she felt about her self-identity into drugs and sex. I believe the frustration about being uncertain about her sexuality in a Catholic school environment may have been the reason Liz acted out.

EMMA

"Emma" was very sweet and a little on the shy side, and we had been friends since grade school. When we were in seventh grade, Emma went through a "scene phase." She chopped off her hair into an unorthodox cut and began layering on very dark gothic style makeup. Emma also stopped listening to regular music and began immersing herself in angry music that was typically inappropriate and very dark. Emma started "seeing" a boy named Jack. She would constantly describe her visits with Jack, which required her lying and sneaking out of the house. As the relationship progressed, the anger and the abnormal negative attitude became much worse. The final issue occurred when Emma ran away from home because Jack requested that she do so. Her family, in a panic, found Emma. They soon discovered that Emma was suffering from stress-related mental health issues and had been self-harming. Thankfully, Emma's parents immediately sought the help of a major mental health hospital, and Emma had to see a psychologist and stay at the hospital for several months. As the family worked through therapy, it became obvious that Emma's parents did not like Jack and forbade her from seeing him, which resulted in Emma's rebellion and depression. Jack attempted suicide, claiming that he was incapable of living without Emma, which in turn increased Emma's guilt. It took a lot of hard work and patience to return Emma to her normal happy and healthy self.

TAYLOR

"Taylor" was a new student in my sixth-grade class. She was a transfer student from a neighboring middle school. She was outgoing and sweet. Taylor lived in a single-mother household because of domestic issues between her parents. Taylor's father had been forced to leave the relationship at the same time that Taylor switched schools. Taylor caught the eye of a boy in our peer group, and although he tried his best to "go out" with Taylor, she did not return the feelings. Tragically, the boy attempted to drown himself in the bathroom at school because of Taylor's denial. We all felt that this weighed heavily on Taylor's mind. Looking back, this was quite an intense situation to cope with mentally at such a young and innocent age. It also can be said that in addition to this near tragedy, Taylor was dealing with home issues that she did not talk about. When her mom decided to move because they could no longer afford the house that Taylor grew up in, Taylor started to steal her mom's alcohol and get drunk. She began to bring liquor to school in a water bottle and drink all day. No one but her closest friends knew, and we tried everything we could to help her. Looking back, we should have told an adult. Perhaps Taylor could have received help earlier, which would have prevented her later mistakes and unplanned pregnancy in high school.

"E"

I met "E" in the seventh grade. She was somewhat of a strange addition to our friend group, which consisted of timid, artistic girls. She was outspoken to the point that it almost seemed like she wanted other people outside of our group to hear and recognize her value. She wore heavy eyeliner and usually dressed in black lace on a daily basis. E didn't show any severe signs of risk-taking behavior until midway through high school. Discussions about her home life were off limits, and we respected that, but definitely wondered why. I had never expected her to run away from home when she was 15, and when this occurred, it was quite a shock. I received an anxious text from her mother on a Saturday night. She was terrified and texting everyone she could find in E's contact list, inquiring if anyone had seen her or knew where she could be. On Monday morning, E was at school wearing a very pretty dress and acting normal, if not giddy. She was telling everyone about how she loved all the attention she was receiving because of her new outfit, especially from the boys. The following year, E began dating many people who did not treat her appropriately. She knew that people were spreading rumors about her, and exteriorly she carried those rumors like a badge of honor. As a teenager, I thought E just liked to be the center of attention, good or bad. As an adult, I wish I had reached out further. I found out 3 years later, once our friend group had disbanded, that E suffered from a very abusive relationship with her father and subsequent male friends. This abuse was directly linked to her oversexualized behaviors. She was dealing with that abuse during freshman year. If our friend group had reached out rather than judged her, we could've supported her and gotten her the help she needed from the school counselor.

SILVIA

I met "Silvia" when I was 7. She didn't start to show strange or risky behaviors or wear strange clothes until high school, which was especially alarming because she had always been conservative and sweet. Silvia showed similar behavior to that of a rebellious teenager, initially. Things with Silvia became stranger and stranger as time progressed during our adolescent years. The strangest occurrence happened when Silvia faked being pregnant multiple times. She also continued her web of lies, claiming that she was being abused by her boyfriend, had a miscarriage, and was homeless. She would wear the same couple of large hoodies to school every day, looking sad and depleted. People would sympathize with her and try to befriend her. Some classmates gave her money or brought her clothes that she accepted. Later, once people started to notice her trend of being pregnant and then miscarrying, her peers wanted nothing to do with her. As a result, people began to mock her, which resulted in multiple fights and a very unhealthy perception of her among our peer group. These strange attention-seeking behaviors were bizarre to us, and I feel that Silvia definitely needed to seek emotional help from a psychiatrist or other trained professional.

YASMINE

"Yasmine" was my best friend from fifth to eighth grade. She was very outspoken and outgoing from the moment I met her. She never wanted to do her schoolwork and often verbally fought with teachers. She got into at least one fight every year in middle school. On the last day of the eighth grade, she fought Sally. After that incident, she was homeschooled, and I never spoke to her again. As I look back on this, I realize that her behavior was most likely because of the bullying she'd dealt with at school. In the fifth grade, she was not as aggressive, but she was mocked in a cruel manner, repeatedly. She was overweight and already suffering from diabetes as a result of the obesity. She used violence to scare people out of bullying her and her friends, and the strategy worked because she never "lost" a fight and was extremely tough, inside and out. I believe that these unpleasant situations could have been avoided had the teachers been more aware of the bullying and abuse, which resulted in her defensive behaviors. Instead, Yasmine was the person who was punished and suspended for fighting, when in reality, she was merely defending herself. The teachers could've reached out more and attempted to investigate deeper into the reasoning behind the reoccurring fights. The teachers labeled her a "bad kid" and never tried to understand what made her feel like she needed to be so aggressive. Usually, the people she fought had teased her about her weight or the fact that she was diabetic, which is cruel and uncalled for. I truly did not blame her for reacting the way she did. A person can only take so much.

MODEL ATHLETE

This example is of a student who was involved in drugs. The person was a model student-athlete, and very kind and caring towards his peers. His father was not involved at all in his life up until high school, and after that, the student began to form a tight-knit relationship with his father. This is around the same time that he started exhibiting behavioral issues. There is no way to tell if his father coming back into his life was the root cause of his behavioral issues, but there is a correlation and a contributing factor. During his second year of high school, the student was arrested at school for possession of marijuana on school grounds. This risk-taking behavior affected his life in a great way and resulted in him moving away from the school district where he grew up. This risk-taking behavior did not have a visible effect on his everyday life. He was still a very popular student-athlete with the same friend group and the same personality.

LARRY

"Larry" was a fourth grader and attended a summer camp enrichment program. Without warning, Larry would act out on random days. He would begin making loud noises and having what seemed like little to no control over his physical actions. During these episodes, it would seem like he was having seizures. Larry would self-injure, hurting himself by banging his head against the wall, throwing himself on the floor, yelling and screaming, and hitting himself. Professionals at the camp were stunned and began to ask if this was severe attention-seeking behavior? Was this an extreme means of getting attention? Was Larry dealing with something at home? It was later understood that the "acting out" behaviors were symptomatic of post-traumatic stress disorder flashbacks concerning Larry being sexually abused as a young child by his older brother. Professional counselors stated that every time the images of his prior abuse entered his mind, they triggered his body to act out of fear of the violence that had been perpetrated against him in the past. These reactions were extremely difficult to manage and prevent. There are other instances where children are sexually abused at home, and because that is the environment they are raised in, they do the same thing at school. Often, victims sexually abuse their peers thinking it is okay to do so when the reality is that abuse is a vicious cycle.

ABUSED ABUSER

A parallel can be drawn to children who are being physically abused at home. An example is that of a student and his risk-taking behavior. In addition, this student physically abused and harmed fellow students at school. He would corner his peers and assault them by means of punching and kicking in order to gain power and intimidate them. As an onlooker, I learned later that this student was being a bully because he was being bullied by his family at home. He was exhibiting this type of behavior toward other people in a school setting because the behavior was deemed appropriate in his household setting. To him, because of the violent environment in which he was immersed, these violent behaviors seemed like normal behavior and not at all inappropriate.

In scenarios where students are exhibiting risk-taking or violent behavior, it is important to assess the root of the issue. If teachers simply punish a student, they may not be fixing what the main causes of the actions are.

MICHELLE

M y good friend growing up, we will call her "Michelle," was a mixed girl. She had two siblings who were fully white, one older and one younger. She lived with her mother and the two siblings. We were friends, and we still see each other on limited occasions. Michelle always had to be seen, heard, and portrayed as the "black girl." She would say things about her mother, who is white, and try to make everything her mother did or said a bad thing. She picked fights with other mixed girls, white girls, and black girls. When we would talk about something like our families or other friends, I would often make a simple statement such as, "Mom and I are going somewhere," and Michelle would reply, "My mom is white, so she doesn't know," or "She's doing that white stuff." Michelle was typically punished for picking fights, in which she was mostly trying to prove that she was "black." Michelle intentionally tried to provoke other girls who were bigger and darker than her to prove something, mainly her "blackness." Honestly, I stopped talking to her for a while because I was uncomfortable. I loved her mom, and I knew she did too. Michelle was only saying bad things about her mother when others were around. I also felt that she had no reason to be mean to the other girls because of the color of their skin. I believe she wasn't happy with herself and had to prove that she was "black." She had to outdo every black girl and intimidate the white and mixed girls. Michelle could have been assisted in avoiding risk-taking behaviors by learning to be comfortable in her skin and by her parents paying more attention to her needs and explaining to her that it is normal to be mixed. I believe I could have assisted her, but I never did because I didn't know where to begin the conversation or how she would react toward me, so I just hung out with her less often.

CLAYTON

We'll call the person I'm going to discuss "Clayton." Clayton was actually one of my close friends in middle school. We grew up together, we both played sports, and we had the same friend group. He started showing signs of risky behavior in seventh grade. Clayton started dating a girl and wasn't afraid of anything. He didn't have great role models growing up; his older brother was an at-risk student. The behaviors started out with small things like pulling stupid pranks or sexting girls. He then turned to smoking weed and drinking alcohol. These behaviors escalated very quickly, and soon the Clayton I knew was engaged in behaviors that previously never would have occurred to him. I think the main reason for these changes was peer pressure from the other kids in our friend group. It also did not help that he found out he had a condition that would not let him play football anymore, which was very difficult for him to process. After high school began, we drifted apart; he was a new person, and I did not want any part of the "new Clayton." I think that there were a couple of things that could have helped him. One would have been having a better group of friends who didn't want to do illegal things. Second, I think that maybe if there had been a teacher or coach in his life who could have helped when he was struggling and had a positive effect on him, than it would have possibly changed the outcome for Clayton.

KATRINA

"Katrina" was a girl I knew in elementary school. She seemed like the most normal girl in the world. She played basketball for the school and was considered one of the popular girls. It seemed like that was also going to be the case once she began high school. But suddenly, Katrina made a 180-degree turn. I am not completely certain about what happened, but I am going to say what I believe is true. She started to date a guy who was involved in illegal activities. This "boyfriend" was an awful influence on her. She stopped hanging out with all of her friends and "fell off the face of the earth." There were rumors that she was having sex with her boyfriend, and as a result, she began to get bullied at school. She eventually stopped coming to school altogether and enrolled in an online school. This was the biggest change I have ever seen someone go through. Katrina dressed differently, in all black, and got tons of piercings and tattoos. I think that if she wasn't pressured into having sex and would have stuck with the "safer" friends, then things would have turned out very differently. Maybe having a good role model who was older would have helped as well. I think her home life was not the best either, which also could have led to some of her problems.

JOHN

I am going to talk about "John." Now, John's story is very different. I did not know him well at all. He was in one of my classes but was very quiet. He took one of the biggest risks someone could have taken at the time. He "came out" as a transgender person and wanted to go through the steps to become a woman. Like I said before, I did not know him very well, but this came as a pretty big surprise to everyone in our school. He did not seem like a person who would be transgender. He liked a lot of things that were considered "boy" things. He liked comic books, was in the band, and had a girlfriend. His actions were very significant. I am not sure what led him to do this, but I do know that it resulted in another situation that was very sad. He decided to take his own life. I think that this had a lot to do with a lack of support from his family. They were very disapproving of what he wanted to do. I think that if they had been more open-minded and given John better support, than he might still be here today.

TOO MUCH PARTYING

I have seen many people in my life shift behaviors and end up going in the wrong direction. One person I know currently is going down the wrong path while in school. He is putting the social aspect of college in front of the academic focus. He tends to go out more than studying and concentrating on his schoolwork work. While in high school, he used to get good grades and focused on his schoolwork work a lot more than he currently does. He was active in sports and seemed to have a lot of friends and a social life, but school was important to him. It wasn't until about senior year that he started slacking off in school and saying "senioritis" was hitting him. His friends started to get into drugs and alcohol, and they partied a lot more than they had before. That was when he started to become more interested in his social life than in school. This was a big change that affected his way of thinking about school and how he prioritized academics. I think that the drugs were a major aspect of change in his life, as he began to smoke, and it has become a habit for him. It seems as though he would rather get high then do anything else. This change has reflected poorly on him in many ways: with his relationship with his parents and, most notably, his grades. I know his parents have tried to help him and keep him on track with his schoolwork, but it is ultimately up to him. If he wants to better himself and get back on the right track with school and getting a degree, then it has to be his decision.

DEBBIE

"Debbie" wasn't the brightest kid in school, but she always tried her hardest and was an excellent soccer player. She was very social and had a lot going for her. During our sophomore year in high school, she and her best friend got into a huge fight and ended up not being friends anymore. This was a major turning point for Debbie in that she lost the majority of her friends. As a result, she ended up making new friends who were a little older and not necessarily like her old friends. It was then that she began skipping classes to hang out with these other friends, which she had never done before. She also started to go to more parties every weekend, drinking, and doing drugs as well. It did not help that her parents didn't look after her and didn't seem to care or notice what she did with her time. It was not until senior year, when something finally switched in her head, that she realized she was heading down the wrong path. Senior year, she got a DUI while coming home from a party. She was on probation, got kicked off the soccer team, and ended up losing even more people in her life. This changed her whole perspective on how she had been living during those past few years. She ended up becoming friends with me again, and all of her old friends, after the whole incident and has really tried to turn things around for herself. I think that her friends helped her change before things got worse. She decided to go to a university that was far from home to get a fresh start. Debbie is now successful and leading a healthy life.

FIRST FAIL

A person I noticed going in the wrong direction was someone I would have never considered capable of choosing the wrong path. She was a very quiet girl in high school and was at the top of the class. It wasn't until college that she decided to go a little crazy. I think that the most important change I saw was when she started dating a certain boy. The boy dropped out of college within the first few months and went out every night of the week. So, she decided that she would go out every night of the week as well, which was a big change from when she was in high school. It ended up that she failed a class, which would have never happened before she met the boy. Another thing that was alarming to see was that she surrounded herself with people just like her boyfriend. I think that since she did not get much exposure in her social life in high school that she was trying to do that in college, but not in a healthy way. I think her parents sensed the problems and tried to help her see that the boyfriend and "his" friends might not be the best choice for her. The fact that she failed a class really hit her hard, and she started seeing less and less of her boyfriend. I think she began to see how bad of an influence he really was on her. I think her friends and family have been a major influence in helping her to see what is truly important in her life.

THE GAMBLER

A family member problem: This particular family member was headed toward disaster. A few behaviors he displayed included secretly becoming involved in gambling, lying about attending college classes and then proceeding to fail said classes, becoming more involved in drinking, and gaining an extreme amount of weight. At first, we (my other family members and I) noticed the weight gain. This was significant, as he was very actively involved in the military and was quite thin after his basic training. Over the course of the next few months, we began noticing a large increase in his weight. This was alarming since he was supposed to be keeping up with his physical training. Next, the lying about attending his college courses came to light after his parents logged onto his blackboard page and noticed failing grades after he stated he was getting As. They then became suspicious and looked through his bank statements and found out that he was also gambling. He became less social and open to us and often remained very private. I think the freedom of becoming an adult and not having strict supervision led to these changes. He often liked to test boundaries growing up, so believing he wouldn't get caught allowed him the opportunity to do the things he wanted without the consequences. Potential supporters included his friends and his family. We could have assisted in this situation more by discussing the real-life consequences of these actions, as well as offering more support, especially with the college aspect, as my family often pushes college as a "non-choice" (meaning its mandatory that we get at least a bachelor's degree), and letting him know that college isn't for everyone and that it would be okay if he didn't get a degree as long as he had a plan in place.

TOO TAN

M y friend's roommate began moving in the wrong direction. She
went from studying well in high school and earning good grades,
to partying and drinking almost every night in college. She would stay
out until 3 or 4 a.m. every night (weekends and weekdays), as well as skip
classes, which she began to fail. She also became very self-conscious about
her looks and began tanning almost every day. I personally believe genetics
and parental observation had something to do with these risky behaviors.
Her mother is an alcoholic and also tans quite often. I think she learned
these behaviors from her mother and is now doing them as well. I believe
also that the transition from high school to college instigated these changes,
as it is hard to adapt to such a drastic change as well as have the amount
of freedom typical of a college student. I witnessed her failing classes,
repeating those classes, and failing those classes a second time. Becoming
obsessed with looking good and going out, as well as drinking almost
every night, was not a healthy start to her college career. Her true friends
could have been a point of support, as well as any professors who witnessed
her failure in their classes. I think her actual friends (the ones who truly
cared about her well-being) could have discussed the risks of what she was
doing and her professors could have discussed the importance of passing
her courses and possibly offered her the counseling services she needed.

TRAGIC DEPRESSION

My friend was a person in my life whom I noticed moving in a very wrong direction. She became very withdrawn from others, drank more, and stopped caring about what she was saying to people. She would often blurt out offensive comments, hurting the ones who cared about her. Her grades also slipped, and she became very lethargic. Prior to this, she was extremely happy. She tried hard in her classes and was an overall great person to be around. The changes I witnessed were extremely alarming, as this was not the person I was used to being around. The factor that led to these drastic changes was that her boyfriend of 3 years tragically passed away in a motorcycle accident. Her family, her other friends, and I were definitely supportive of her. I often tried to listen to her grieving. I offered my shoulder to cry on and talked her through the situation. I gave her as much support and praise as I could offer, and when the time was right (after she stated that she might want to get professional help), I even offered to go with her if she needed it. I truly just think having some peers around to support you through such a difficult time helps the situation tremendously.

SPIRAL OUT OF CONTROL

M y best friend from high school used to do well in school and was a very nice person. During his junior year, he started drinking and stopped going to class. He turned into a very mean person and was always fighting about things, like money. The drinking turned into an out of control situation. I think that if someone close to him, like a family, had warned him about the risks of developing an alcohol addiction, he might be in a different situation today.

EIGHTH-GRADE PROBLEMS

One of my good friends in middle school was always happy and having a great and healthy time. He seemed to enjoy school and was on the football team. In eighth grade, he began smoking pot and partying. He went to high school online and became very emotionally unstable. I know that he was involved in multiple fights and even went to jail as a result, for assault. I think that if his parents had been stricter regarding him doing drugs, his life could have turned out differently and healthier.

ABUSE AND RETURN

A girl I went to high school with was in a physically abusive relationship. The girl was able to break up with the abuser, and shortly afterward, she found out she was pregnant. She decided to abort the baby to make sure that the abuser could never hurt her child. After all of that, she decided to get back together with the abuser. She was very distant and cold to others when her boyfriend was around; she would have bruises on her body and continued to act standoffish when around other males. Yes, she started to let the abuser run her life. Friends and family could have assisted her with breaking ties with the abuser and encouraged her to attend therapy to discuss her abusive relationship and how to cope with that stress. This person needed professional assistance to work through the trauma of the relationship.

OLDER BROTHER, BAD HABITS

O ne of my peers from high school went through some dramatic changes during our junior year. Before anything changed, he was a straight-A student who was active in the band and choir, and participated in cross-country. He was well liked by everyone and had plans to go to college and eventually med school. One change I witnessed was in the fall of our junior year; he began abusing drugs, such as alcohol, marijuana, and tobacco. A second change was that his grades began to slip to Cs and Ds. A third change was that he was less social and surrounded himself with drug abusers. These changes were dramatic and eventually lead to him not going to college and working at an auto parts store. I believe the drugs began because his older brother had tried some, which became a habit. Shortly afterward, my peer began using drugs very frequently and then all the changes started happening. His family could have helped by reducing the exposure he had to his older brother. His friends could have helped by trying to keep him away from the bad influences at school.

REFERENCES

Arnette, J. J. (2016). *Human development: A cultural approach.* New York, New York: Pearson.

Jette, J. E. & Killham, K. M. (2016). *Real-life issues of tweens and teens: A human development perspective.* New York, New York: Pearson.

CPSIA information can be obtained
at www.ICGtesting.com
Printed in the USA
BVHW031941110920
588617BV00004B/310